The
African Grey

An Owner's Guide To

A HAPPY HEALTHY PET

Howell Book House

Howell Book House
A Simon & Schuster Macmillan Company
1633 Broadway
New York, NY 10019

Macmillan Publishing books may be purchased for business or sales promotional use. For information please write: Special Markets Department, Macmillan Publishing USA, 1633 Broadway, New York, NY 10019.

MACMILLAN is a registered trademark of Macmillan, Inc.
Library of Congress Cataloging-in-Publication Data
Rach, Julie.
The African Grey / by Julie Rach.
p. cm.—(An owner's guide to a happy healthy pet)

ISBN 0-87605-443-2

1. African grey parrot   I. Title.   II. Series.
SF473.P3R324   1998
636.6'865—dc21   97–31329
                                                         CIP

Manufactured in the United States of America
10 9 8 7 6 5 4 3 2 1

Series Director: Amanda Pisani
Series Assistant Director: Jennifer Liberts
Book Design: Michele Laseau
Cover Design: Iris Jeromnimon
Illustration: Laura Robbins
Photography:
    Front cover photo by Eric Ilasenko; back cover photo by Mary Bloom
    Joan Balzarini: 16, 20, 72, 104, 108, 119, 120, 125
    Mary Bloom: 46, 49, 65, 69, 98, 102
    Eric Ilasenko: Title page, 2–3, 5, 11, 17, 24, 29, 31, 33, 35, 39, 44, 55, 56, 60,
        63, 64, 73, 76, 82, 100–101, 103, 105, 107, 114, 116, 118, 122
    Julie Rach: 26, 27, 40, 48, 52, 110
    David Schilling: 10, 13, 38, 66
    Faith Uridel: 12, 51
    B. Everett Webb: 7, 8, 19, 22–23, 25, 37, 43, 57, 59, 61, 74
Production Team: Stephanie Hammett, Natalie Hollifield, Clint Lahnen,
    Dennis Sheehan, Terri Sheehan, Chris Van Camp

Contents

Welcome
to the
World

of the

African
Grey

External Features of the African Grey

Crown

Cere

Eye Ring

Nare

Nape

Beak

Mantle

Wing

Breast

Tail Feathers (Retrices)

chapter 1

The African Grey's Ancestry

At this time, scientists have identified about 750 parrot species. Of this impressive number, about 280 are kept as pets, and about 250 of those have bred successfully in captivity, assuring that parrots will be around for future generations to appreciate. Since birds have been kept as pets for centuries, prospective bird owners will find themselves in good company historically.

Birdkeeping Through the Ages

The ancient Egyptians are credited with being the first to keep birds, most notably pigeons. Queen Hatsheput (1504 to 1482 B.C.) was credited as being the first monarch to create a royal zoo, which

Welcome to the
World of the
African Grey

included exotic birds. The ancient Persians also knew of talking birds as early as the fifth century B.C., when a court physician and naturalist wrote about talking birds described to him by Indian merchants.

CLASSICAL GREECE AND ROME

From Egypt, birdkeeping spread to Greece and Rome. Some historians credit Alexander the Great with discovering the Alexandrian parakeet, and the Greeks receive credit for popularizing parrot-keeping outside the birds' native lands of Africa and Asia. In the first century A.D., Pliny the Elder taught parrot training and suggested that each bird be housed in a darkened room to help it learn to speak.

Wealthy Romans built elaborate garden aviaries, and they also used mockingbirds in the entryways of their homes as feathered doorbells to announce visitors. The Romans are thought to be the first bird dealers, bringing different types of birds to Great Britain and the European continent.

EUROPE

Although birdkeeping was still largely an upper-class fancy, the Renaissance opened it up as a hobby for the masses. Portuguese sailors introduced Europe to canaries at this time, and in the 1600s the Dutch began producing varieties of canaries for show. These birds were exported to Britain, where birdkeeping became quite popular.

Around this time, in the British penal colony of Australia, a forger named Thomas Watling first described the budgerigar's ability to mimic human speech. This bird greeted Watling's employer by saying, "How do you do, Dr. White?"

Birdkeeping as we know it today can be traced to its beginning in Victorian Great Britain, when bird sellers in the British Isles would offer goldfinches and larks to ship captains en route to the West Indies. These common European birds would then be traded in the islands for species found there.

Some notable bird owners of history include King Henry VIII, whose African grey was alleged to have called for help when he fell in the Thames River; Marie Antoinette, who also had an African grey parrot; Wolfgang Amadeus Mozart, who kept canaries and a pet starling; Thomas Jefferson, who made a pet of a mockingbird; Andrew Jackson, whose parrot, Polly, made life interesting at the White House; and Theodore Roosevelt, whose family kept a Hyacinth Macaw during their stay in the White House.

The African Grey's Background

As his name implies, the African grey parrot is a gray bird that comes from Africa. Attractive gray birds with red tails were seen around 1402 in the Canary Islands. They had been imported from West Africa. To this day, African greys are found in western and central Africa, from Guinea to northern Angola. The British spelling of grey is used in connection with these birds because British sailors and explorers were among the first to bring African greys out of the jungle and make pets of them.

Two subspecies have been identified: the Congo grey and the Timneh grey. Both species have featherless white faces and eyes that change color as the birds

Greys were taken from jungles and first domesticated by British sailors and explorers.

mature. Birds under six months of age have large dark eyes, while birds between six months and one year of age have light gray eyes. Year-old birds have beige eyes and birds over the age of two have eyes with yellow irises and black pupils.

THE CONGO GREY

The Congo grey *(Psittacus erithacus)* is a gray bird with a solid black beak and a bright red tail. He measures

Welcome to the
World of the
African Grey

about 12 to 14 inches in length and weighs between 450 and 500 grams or about a pound. Congos reach maturity when they are about two years old and can live to be fifty.

You may hear your bird's breeder mention a Ghana or West African subspecies. These birds aren't a true subspecies, but rather are smaller, darker Congos that average 10 inches in length and weigh between 350 and 400 grams (about ³/₄ of a pound).

THE TIMNEH GREYS

Timneh greys (*Psittacus erithacus timneh*) are smaller, darker birds with maroon tails and, and their black beaks have a pinkish cast. They measure about 10 inches in length and weigh about 300 grams (about 10 ounces). They reach maturity at about age two and can live fifty years.

Other than size and coloring, there's very little difference between the two subspecies. Some people consider the Timneh to be an inferior pet, but that isn't so at all.

The Congo grey (left) is larger with lighter coloring than the Timneh grey (right).

African greys are found in western and central Africa, from Guinea to northern Angola. The Congo, also called the Cameroon or Ghana grey, ranges from Cote d'Ivoire to northern Angola, while the Timneh is found in southern Guinea and western Cote d'Ivoire. The birds live in mangrove swamps and along rivers, foraging for fruits, nuts, seeds and berries. They also raid cultivated crops.

A Swiss naturalist first described African greys in the 1500s saying, "I also have one that is ash-colored or light blue over its whole body, except on the tail alone it has red feathers, and around the eyes it is white." African greys were first identified by naturalist Carolus Linnaeus in 1758, making them one of the first parrot species to be scientifically classified. They were introduced in England by King Henry VII in the early 1500s. King Henry's pet grey is reported to have called out "Help! I am drowning!" when he fell into the Thames River during a royal outing.

The African grey kept by the Duchess of Richmond and Lennox, who was also the mistress of Charles II of England, was buried with her in Westminster Abbey. He can be seen there today as the oldest surviving example of avian taxidermy. Marie Antoinette received a grey as a gift, and Queen Victoria's grey, Coco, had a vocabulary that included "God save the Queen!"

PARROT TRAITS
The African grey is a type of parrot, just like the Hyacinth Macaw or Mealy Amazon. The traits that all parrot species have in common are:
• four toes—two pointing backward and two pointing forward
• upper beak overhanging the lower
• broad head and short neck
However, a healthy African grey measures about 11 inches to 13½ inches from head to tip of the tail, while a full-grown Scarlet Macaw can easily reach 40 inches in length.

Greys were first bred outside of Africa in 1770 when a pair were coupled in France for breeding purposes. A British pair of pet birds followed suit in the United Kingdom in 1843. This pair of birds successfully raised a single chick after the breeder fashioned a flannel nest for the hen.

GREYS IN AMERICA

The grey's history in the United States has also gone largely unrecorded. We do know that one of the first successful breeders of African greys in the United States set up a colony breeding situation in a cow barn in 1903. When he checked on the colony three years later, the breeder reported finding sixty-seven additional birds and eleven skeletons. His initial results

Welcome to the
World of the
African Grey

were met with skepticism, and he retired from parrot breeding until the 1930s, when he again began to breed greys, but under more traditional circumstances.

Until about twenty years ago, most of the pet greys in the United States were imported from Africa. The situation began changing in the 1980s, when stricter importing regulations began to be enacted. By the early 1990s, almost no African greys were being brought into the United States, thanks to a combination of international laws and a reluctance on the part of airlines that once carried large shipments of birds to become involved in the now-complicated import process.

African greys are a type of parrot and share similar traits, such as a broad head and short neck.

The Amazing Alex

In 1977, Irene Pepperberg, PhD, purchased an African grey parrot in a Chicago pet store as part of a research project to examine animal intelligence and communication skills.

That bird is Alex, and he has proved to be an exceptional research subject. Dr. Pepperberg has learned that Alex not only uses human language to communicate, but he uses language appropriately, noting differences and similarities in objects that are shown to him, and telling researchers the colors and materials these objects are made from.

Alex was joined in the lab by two African grey chicks in 1992. These birds began by identifying objects, such as paper or cork. This was followed by them learning the concept of category, including the number of a particular item, its relative size, the material it is made from and its color. Finally, the birds learned phonemes (distinctive sounds) and how to combine them.

Alex and the other birds in Dr. Pepperberg's lab are not the first African greys studied in this manner. Researchers in Europe developed a method of communicating with African greys in the 1940s and 1950s, and a German researcher popularized the use of the model/rival technique to teach and study African grey parrots. In this method, the teacher shows one of two students (either avian or human) an object and asks what it is. If the student identifies it correctly, the teacher gives the object to the student to examine and play with. If the student gives an incorrect answer, the teacher and the other student "model" the correct response, then the teacher asks the first student the question again. Tests conducted on Alex indicate that he can answer eighty percent of the questions asked him correctly.

African greys have shown the ability to use human language to communicate.

Alex knows the names of almost one hundred items, he can count to six, he can name about seven colors and about seven different types of materials. He has also made up his own names for some items, such as "banana cracker" to describe a banana chip, "cork nut" to ask for an almond in its shell and "rock corn" to distinguish dried corn from fresh.

chapter 2

African Greys
as Pets

For the last nine years I have been owned by an African grey parrot. Sindbad joined my home as the importation of wild-caught parrots was ending. Feather-picked from her neck to her vent and brain damaged to the point of seizures, she was a skinny, frightened creature when I first saw her. Now, as she sits on my desk, it seems impossible that this fully feathered creature who is in control of her faculties and filled out to the point of plumpness can be the same bird.

Sindbad and I began modifying each other's behavior from the start, although her attempts were more subtle than mine. As I changed her diet from primarily sunflower seeds with few fruits to a smorgasbord of fresh produce and other healthful treats, she taught

12

me to respond day or night to her insistent beak tapping on the side of her cage when she'd fallen from her perch and couldn't climb back up. I encouraged her to play by providing her with a variety of safe and interesting toys, and she got me to laugh when she bulldozed them off her cage and onto the floor with the subtlety of a Sherman tank at full throttle. I improved her health with a better diet and frequent trips to the veterinarian, and she improved mine with her amusing antics.

Things African Grey Owners Need to Know

Greys are good choices for owners who cannot tolerate consistent loud noise, according to longtime parrot fancier Arthur Freud. Based on my experience with Sindbad, I must agree. She is much quieter than the cockatoos, macaws or Amazons I have been around. Also, she can be persuaded to quiet down more quickly than some of her more vocal feathered friends by covering her cage with a beach towel or by distracting her with a toy or a treat.

African greys need a variety of interesting toys to keep them mentally stimulated.

IF YOU HAVE ALLERGIES

African greys are dusty birds. Their feather dander and dust from their powder down feathers can cause or aggravate allergies. Symptoms can include sneezing, nasal congestion and itchy, watery eyes in sensitive people.

GREYS HAVE SMARTS

African greys are intelligent pets. Researchers have estimated that they are as intelligent as dolphins, chimps and even toddlers, depending on the intelligence criteria being studied. Grey parrots can use that intelligence for good activities—becoming charming talkative pets—or

Welcome to the
World of the
African Grey

they can turn it against themselves—becoming nail biters or feather pullers.

Partly because of this intelligence, African greys can be demanding pets. They require consistent attention from their owners, along with an interesting environment that includes some positive mental challenges, such as a wide variety of interesting toys, to keep them stimulated.

ABOUT THE TIME COMMITMENT

David Alderton may have summarized African grey ownership accurately in his book *A Birdkeeper's Guide to Pet Birds* when he wrote, "You should only contemplate obtaining one of these parrots if you are able to devote considerable time and attention to it. In return, you should have a lifelong companion, since grey parrots will live for decades." I admit it: I have devoted a good bit of the last nine years of my life to one small grey parrot. However, the return I receive on that investment is a reasonably healthy, fully feathered, charming companion who rewards me with entertaining antics and unconditional love. I think I've come out far ahead on my end of the bargain.

To illustrate how much time an African grey takes, let me outline my morning schedule: After I've had my shower, I come downstairs and let Sindbad out of her cage. I remove her evening food and water bowls and hold her over the trash can so she can defecate. While I'm waiting for her to take care of business, I pet her head and rub under her wings. Not only does she get attention this way, but it's also the perfect opportunity for me to check her over for lumps, bumps, scrapes, ingrown feathers and anything else that seems out of the ordinary.

After Sindbad has relieved herself, I put her on top of her cage and make her breakfast. On a good day, the routine that precedes my making her breakfast takes twenty minutes. If she's feeling neglected or in need of more attention than usual, it can take a half hour or more. Then I chop her fruits and vegetables, add them to the Nutriberries and almonds I've already placed in her bowl and serve the meal to Sindbad. While I make my own breakfast and finish getting ready, she's left atop her cage to play for another thirty minutes or so until it's time for me to leave.

I usually come home for lunch to give her some out time at midday, then she expects more time out of her cage before dinner and as much attention as I will give her in the evenings. This can be as simple as having her sit next to me while I'm reading or watching TV or as involved as an extensive cuddling session in which I help her preen hard-to-reach feathers. All in all, Sindbad gets a minimum of two hours of attention from me each day—and that's about as little as an African grey can stand. She'd like considerably more time, believe me, but it's difficult to fit more than that in consistently.

DIETARY CONSIDERATIONS

African greys need higher levels of calcium in their diets than other parrot species. If they don't receive enough calcium from their diets, their bodies will remove calcium from their bones, which can leave greys vulnerable to fractures. You can provide your grey with adequate amounts of dietary calcium by sprinkling a high-quality calcium powder on your pet's fresh foods; by offering her small amounts of calcium-rich foods, such as cheese or yogurt; or by giving her mineral blocks or cuttlebone to chew on.

African greys can be somewhat fussy eaters. As a rule, Sindbad is automatically suspicious of any new food that appears in her bowl. She usually acclimates to new foods within several days of seeing the food for the first time. Her tastes also run somewhat hot and cold. What seems to be her first and most favorite choice one week can be easily passed over in favor of another morsel on the following week.

PERSONALITY TRAITS

African greys can be shy around strangers. If you want a boisterous parrot that will show off readily and

Welcome to the
World of the
African Grey

perform tricks, a grey may not be the ideal choice for you.

Every time Sindbad meets someone new or sees a friend who hasn't stopped by in awhile, she sits on the floor of her cage still as a statue and shakes slightly. After she realizes that the person means her no harm, she begins to chirp quietly or fluff her feathers in greeting.

African greys aren't fond of baths. They keep their feathers in condition by preening and with the powder down that comes from their undercoat of white, fluffy feathers.

Your grey may be shy—give her time to warm up to new people.

African greys can become one-person birds. If they are not properly socialized to being handled by all family members, they can become overly attached to whomever feeds them and cleans their cage. Some would say greys tend to bond to only one person, but I would disagree with that. Sindbad was formerly a "man's bird" who didn't want to have much to do with women, and children terrified her. Since coming to live with me, she has been handled by both my male and female friends and her male and female animal health technicians and veterinarians. She didn't seem to favor one gender over the other, and even learned to tolerate gentle attention from one of my veterinarian's children.

African greys are clumsy, particularly when they are chicks. Make your grey feel more comfortable when you hold her or carry her by allowing her to rest her beak on your chest as she perches on your hand. Many birds feel more secure when they are held or carried in this manner.

EXPENSES OF BIRD OWNERSHIP

And finally, the all-important costs of grey ownership. When considering the purchase of an African grey, you must factor in the following up-front expenses: the cost of the bird; the cost of her cage and accessories; the cost of bird food, including seeds or formulated diets and fresh foods; the cost of toys; and the cost of veterinary care. The last three items are ongoing costs and must be considered over the course of forty or fifty years, which is how long African grey parrots can live.

To give you an idea of the annual upkeep on an African grey, here's what I spend on Sindbad in an average year: at least $1,500 on food and toys (average $30 a week for Nutriberries, fresh produce and chewable toys), $600 to $1,000 on veterinary care, and $150 to $200 on boarding. Because she was a wild-caught bird and has chronic health problems, her vet bills are considerably higher than what you can expect to pay for a domestically bred bird raised in this country. Still, it would not be extraordinary to spend $2,000 a year on a well-cared-for grey.

A healthy African grey has bright eyes and a full-chested appearance.

Where Will You Get Your Grey?

Greys can be purchased through several sources, including bird breeders, who will advertise in bird specialty magazines, the pet section of your newspaper's

Welcome to the
World of the
African Grey

classified ads or on the Internet; bird shows and marts, which offer breeders and buyers an opportunity to get together and share their love of birds; and bird specialty stores. Once you've located a source for African greys, it's time to get down to the all-important task of selecting your pet.

Look at the birds that are available for sale. If possible, sit down and watch them for awhile. Don't rush this important step. Do some of them seem bolder than the others? Consider those first, because you want a curious, active, robust pet, rather than a shy animal that hides in a corner.

If possible, let your grey choose you. Many bird stores display their livestock on T-stands or playgyms, or a breeder may bring out a clutch of babies for you to look at. If one bird waddles right up to you and wants to play, or if one comes over to check you out and just seems to want to come home with you, that's the bird you want!

SIGNS OF A HEALTHY GREY

Here are some of the indicators of a healthy grey. Keep them in mind when selecting your pet, and reject any birds that do not meet these criteria.

- bright eyes
- a clean cere (the area above the bird's beak that covers her nares or nostrils)
- upright posture
- a full-chested appearance
- actively moving around the cage
- clean legs and vent
- smooth feathers
- good appetite

THE PREOWNED PARROT

As you make your selection of the right African grey for you, you may see adult birds advertised for sale at a bird store or in the newspaper. Adopting an adult grey could be a great mistake (if the bird has a number of behavioral problems), or she could the best investment you'll ever make.

People put adult greys up for sale for many reasons. Perhaps the bird detects stress in the home and begins to pull her feathers, and the owners have neither the time nor the patience to solve the problem. The owners may have a child and suddenly not have time for the parrot or they may be moving and cannot take their pet with them. Some people simply lose interest in their birds and sell them after a few years.

My results with a previously owned grey have been completely satisfying, but it has required a considerable investment of time, patience and money to restore Sindbad's health and allow her charming personality to come through. I can't guarantee that you'll find a diamond in the rough like I did when I adopted my adult grey, but I would certainly encourage you to consider an adult bird when you're looking for a pet.

Bringing Your Grey Home

Give your grey a chance to adjust to your family's routine gradually after you bring her home. Your new pet will need some time to adjust to her new environment, so be patient. After you set your grey up in her cage for the first time, spend a few minutes talking quietly to your new pet, and use her name frequently while you're talking. Describe the room she is living in, or tell her about your family.

After a few days, you will notice that your grey has her own routine.

YOUR GREY'S ROUTINE

After a couple of days of adjustment, your grey should start to settle into her routine. You will be able to tell when your new pet has adjusted to your home, because healthy greys will spend about equal amounts of time during the day eating, playing, sleeping and defecating. By observation, you will soon recognize your pet's

Welcome to the
World of the
African Grey

normal routine. You may also notice that your bird fluffs or shakes her feathers to greet you, or that she chirps a greeting when you uncover her cage in the morning.

Don't become alarmed the first time you see your grey asleep. Although it seems that your bird has lost her head or a leg, she's fine. Sleeping on one foot with its head tucked under her wing (actually with her head turned about 180 degrees and her beak tucked into the feathers on the back of her neck) is a normal sleeping position for many parrots, although it looks a bit unusual or uncomfortable to bird owners. Be aware, too, that your bird will occasionally perch on one leg while resting

Don't be alarmed if your African grey perches on one leg while resting or eating something interesting.

Greys and Children

African greys and children can get along well in a household if parents remind children of the following rules when they're around the parrot:

1. Approach the cage quietly. Birds don't like to be surprised. Say the bird's name softly to let her know you're in the room.
2. Talk softly to the bird. Don't scream or yell at her.
3. Don't shake or hit the cage.
4. Don't poke at the bird or her cage with your fingers, sticks, pencils or other items. Birds will defend their homes and will bite at intruding items, including fingers.
5. If you're allowed to take the bird out of her cage, handle her gently.
6. Don't take the bird outside. In unfamiliar surroundings (such as the outdoors), birds can become confused and fly away from their owners. Most are never recovered.
7. Respect the bird's need for quiet time.

You can involve children in caring for your African grey. Although the bird may be "a family pet," each family member can be responsible for some aspect of the bird's care, such as changing the cage papers, replacing water and food bowls with fresh offerings or playing with the parrot when she's on a playgym. Even the youngest family members can help out by selecting healthful foods for the bird on a trip to the market or picking out a safe, colorful toy at the bird store.

I'd like to remind adults to please not give any live pet to a child or to your family as a holiday present. Birthdays, Christmas, Hanukkah and other holidays are exciting, but stressful, times for both people and animals. A pet bird coming to a new home is under enough stress just by joining her new family; don't add to her stress by bringing her home for a holiday.

Living

with an

part two

African Grey

chapter 3

Caring
for Your
African Grey

Ten Steps to Better Bird Care

Despite what you may think, bird keeping isn't particularly difficult. In fact, if you only do ten things for your grey for as long as you own him, your bird will have a pretty healthy, well-adjusted life. Each step will be discussed in more detail in subsequent chapters, but here they are in a brief summary:

First, **provide a safe, secure cage in a safe, secure location** in your home. This cage should have appropriate-sized bar spacing and cage accessories that are designed for greys, and the cage should be located in a fairly active part of your home (the family room, for example) so your bird will feel as if he's part of your family and your daily routine.

Next, **clean the cage regularly** to protect your pet from illness and to make his surroundings more enjoyable for both of you. Would you want to live in a smelly, dirty house? Your bird doesn't like it either.

Third, **clip your bird's wings regularly** to ensure his safety. Also bird-proof your home and practice bird safety by closing windows and doors securely before you let your bird out of his cage, keeping your bird indoors when he isn't caged and ensuring that your pet doesn't chew on anything harmful (from houseplants to leaded glass lampshades to power cords) or become poisoned by toxic fumes from overheated nonstick cookware, cleaning products and other household products.

A varied diet including seeds, fresh vegetables, fruits and healthy people food will keep your African grey healthy.

Fourth, **offer your grey a varied diet** that includes seeds or pellets, fresh vegetables and fruits cut into small portions, and healthy people food, such as raw or cooked pasta, fresh or toasted whole-wheat bread and unsweetened breakfast cereals.

In addition to giving your grey good, healthy foods, don't feed your pet chocolate, alcohol, avocado or highly sugared, salted or fatty foods. Provide the freshest food possible, and remove partially eaten or discarded food from the cage before it has a chance to spoil and make your pet sick. Your grey should also have access to clean, fresh drinking water at all times.

Next, establish a good working relationship with a **qualified avian veterinarian** early on in your bird ownership (preferably on your way home from the pet store or breeder). Don't wait for an emergency to locate a veterinarian.

Sixth, take your grey to the veterinarian for **regular checkups,** as well as when you notice a change in his routine. Illnesses in birds are sometimes difficult to detect before it's too late to save the bird, so preventive care helps head off serious problems before they develop.

Seventh, **set and maintain a routine** for your grey. Make sure he's fed at about the same time each day, his playtime out of his cage occurs regularly and that his bedtime is well established.

Eighth, provide an **interesting environment** for your bird. Make him feel that he's part of your family. Entertain and challenge your bird's curiosity with a variety of safe toys. Rotate these toys in and out of your bird's cage regularly, and discard any that become soiled, broken, frayed, worn or otherwise unsafe.

Female pet greys sometimes lay eggs, much to their owners' surprise.

Ninth, **leave a radio or television on for your bird when you are away** from home, because a too-quiet environment can be stressful for many birds, and stress can cause illness or other problems for your pet.

Finally, **pay attention to your grey on a consistent basis.** Don't lavish abundant attention on the bird when you first bring him home, then gradually lose interest in him. Birds are sensitive, intelligent creatures that will not understand such a mixed message. Set aside a portion of each day to spend with your grey—you'll both enjoy it and your relationship will benefit from it. Besides, wasn't companionship one of the things you were looking for when you picked your grey as a pet?

Now that doesn't seem too difficult, does it? Just devote a little time each day to your pet bird, and soon the two of you will have formed a lifelong bond of trust and mutual enjoyment.

A Routine for You and Your Grey

Your grey requires a certain level of care each day to ensure his health and well-being. Here are some of the things you'll need to do each day for your pet:

- Observe your pet for any changes in his routine (report any changes to your avian veterinarian immediately).

- Offer fresh food and remove old food. Wash food dish thoroughly with detergent and water. Rinse thoroughly and allow to dry.

- Check seed dish and refill as necessary with clean, fresh seed.

- Provide fresh water and remove previous dish. Wash dish as above.

- Change paper in cage tray.

- Let the bird out of his cage for supervised playtime.

- Finally, you'll want to cover your bird's cage at about the same time every night to indicate bedtime. Greys seem to thrive when they have a familiar routine. When you cover the cage, you'll probably hear your bird rustling around for a while, perhaps getting a drink of water or a last mouthful of seeds

Your grey should be given fresh, healthful food every day.

27

before settling in for the night. Keep in mind that your pet will require eight to ten hours of sleep a day, but you can expect that he will take naps during the day to supplement his nightly snooze.

BE ALERT TO HEALTH INDICATORS

Although it may seem a bit unpleasant to discuss, your bird's droppings require daily monitoring because they can tell you a lot about his general health. Greys produce white-and-green tubular droppings. These droppings are usually composed of equal amounts of fecal material (the green portion), urine (a clear liquid portion) and urates (the white or cream-colored part). A healthy grey generally eliminates about every forty minutes, although your bird may go more or less often.

Texture and consistency, along with frequency or lack of droppings, can let you know how your pet is feeling. For instance, if a bird eats a lot of fruits and vegetables, his droppings are generally looser and more watery than a bird that eats primarily seeds. But watery droppings can also indicate illness, such as diabetes or kidney problems, that cause a bird to drink more water than usual.

Color can also give an indication of health. Birds that have psittacosis (a relatively common and very contagious disease of pet birds that usually involves the digestive tract—also known as "parrot fever") typically have bright, lime-green droppings, while healthy birds have avocado or darker green and white droppings. Birds with liver problems may produce droppings that are yellowish or reddish, while birds that have internal bleeding will produce dark, tarry droppings.

But a color change doesn't necessarily indicate poor health. For instance, birds that eat pelleted diets tend

---

WARM WEATHER WARNING

On a warm day, you may notice your bird sitting with his wings held away from his body, rolling his tongue and holding his mouth open. This is how a bird cools himself off. Watch your bird carefully on warm days because he can overheat quickly and may suffer heatstroke, which requires veterinary care. If you live in a warm climate, ask your avian veterinarian how you can protect your bird from this potentially serious problem.

to have darker droppings than their seed-eating companions, while parrots that have splurged on a certain fresh food soon have droppings with that characteristic color. Birds that overindulge on beets, for instance, produce bright red droppings that can look as though the bird has suffered some serious internal injury. Other birds that overdo sweet potatoes, blueberries or raspberries produce orange, blue or red droppings. During pomegranate season, Sindbad's droppings take on a decidedly violet hue that alarmed me greatly the first few times I saw them.

As part of your daily cage cleaning and observation of your feathered friend, look at his droppings carefully. Learn what is normal for your bird in terms of color, consistency and frequency, and report any changes to your avian veterinarian promptly.

Check your grey's toys every week for signs of excessive wear.

WEEKLY CHORES

Some of your weekly chores will include:

Removing old food from cage bars and from the corners of the cage where it invariably falls.

Removing, scraping and replacing the perches to keep them clean and free of debris. (You might also want to sand them lightly with coarse grain sandpaper to clean them further and improve perch traction for your pet.)

Rotating toys in your bird's cage to keep them interesting. Remember to discard any toys that show excessive signs of wear (frayed rope, cracked plastic or well-chewed wood).

You can simplify the weekly cage cleaning process by placing the cage in the shower and letting hot water from the shower head do some of the work. Be sure to remove your bird, his food and water dishes, the cage tray paper and his toys before putting the cage into the shower. You can let the hot water run over the cage for a few minutes, then scrub at any stuck-on food with an old toothbrush or some fine-grade steel wool. After you've removed the food and other debris, you can disinfect the cage with a spray-on disinfectant that you can purchase at your pet store. Make sure to choose a bird-safe product, and read the instructions fully before use.

Rinse the cage thoroughly and dry it completely before returning your bird and his accessories to the cage. (If you have wooden perches in the cage, you can dry them more quickly by placing the wet dowels in a 400-degree oven for 10 minutes. Let the perches cool before you put them back in the cage.)

HOLIDAY PRECAUTIONS

The holidays are exciting, frenzied and at times stressful. They can also be hazardous to your African grey's health. Drafts from frequently opening and closing doors can have an impact on your bird's health, and the bustle of a steady stream of visitors can add to your pet's stress level.

Chewing on holiday plants, such as poinsettia, holly and mistletoe, can make your bird sick, as can chewing on tinsel or ornaments. Round jingle-type bells can sometimes trap a curious bird's toe, beak or tongue, so keep these holiday decorations out of your bird's reach. Watch your pet around strings of lights, too, as both the bulbs and the cords can prove to be great temptations to curious beaks.

WHEN THE SEASONS CHANGE

Warm weather requires extra vigilance on the part of a pet bird owner to ensure that your pet remains comfortable. To keep your pet cool, keep him out of direct sun, offer him lots of fresh, juicy vegetables and fruits (remove these fresh foods from the cage promptly to prevent your bird from eating spoiled food) and mist him lightly with a clean spray bottle (filled with water only) that is used solely for birdie showers.

Warm weather may also bring out a host of insect pests to bedevil you and your bird. Depending on where you live, you may see ants, mosquitoes or other bugs around your bird's cage as the temperature rises. Take care to keep your bird's cage scrupulously clean to discourage any pests, and remove any fresh foods promptly to keep insects out of your bird's food bowl. Finally, in cases of severe infestation, you may have to use Camicide or other bird-safe insecticides to reduce the insect population. (Remove your bird from the area of infestation before spraying.) If the problem becomes severe enough to require professional exter-

*When the weather
is cool, remember
to provide a com-
fortably warm
location for your
grey.*

minators, make arrangements to have your bird out of the house for at least twenty-four hours after spraying has taken place.

By the same token, pay attention to your pet's needs when the weather turns cooler. You may want to use a heavier cage cover, especially if you lower the heat in your home at bedtime, or you may want to move the bird's cage to another location in your home that is warmer and less drafty.

Moving with Greys

If moving is in your future, you will need to take your grey on a trip, whether it's across town, across a state line or into another country. Your first step should be to acclimate your bird to traveling in the car. Some pet birds take to this new adventure immediately, while others become so stressed out by the trip that they become carsick. Patience and persistence are usually the keys to success if your pet falls into the latter category.

ROAD TRIPS

To get your grey used to riding in the car, start by taking his cage (with door and cage tray well secured) out to your car and placing it inside. Make sure that your car is cool before you do this, because your grey can suffer heatstroke if you place him in a hot car and leave him there.

When your bird seems comfortable sitting in his cage in your car, take him for a short drive, such as around the block. If your bird seems to enjoy the ride (he eats, sings, whistles, talks and generally acts like nothing is wrong), then you have a willing traveler on your hands. If he seems distressed by the ride (he sits on the floor of his cage shaking, screams or vomits), then you have a bit of work ahead of you.

Distressed birds often only need to be conditioned that car travel can be fun. You can do this by talking to your bird throughout the trip. Praise him for good behavior and reassure him that everything will be fine. Offer special treats and juicy fruits (grapes, apples or citrus fruit) so that your pet will eat and will also take in water. On long trips, you may want to remove your pet's water dish during travel to avoid spillage. If you do take out the dish, make sure to stop frequently and give your bird water so he doesn't dehydrate.

As your bird becomes accustomed to car travel, gradually increase the length of the trips. When your bird is comfortable with car rides, begin to condition him for the move by packing your car as you would on moving day. If, for example, you plan to place duffel bags near your bird's cage, put the bags and the cage in the back of the car for a "practice run" before you actually begin the move so your bird can adjust to the size, shape and color of the bags. A little planning on your part will result in a well-adjusted avian traveler and a reduced stress level for you both.

Sindbad enjoys car trips immensely. She used to enjoy them even more when I would put her cage on the front passenger seat of my car. She could climb up into the corner of her cage closest to me and watch me drive. I think she also used to enjoy the feeling of the air conditioning blowing through her feathers. However, after giving the matter some thought, I believe she is safer riding in the back seat of my compact sedan, so that's where she has traveled for much of the last four years. I try to place her cage behind the passenger seat so she can still see me and I can keep an eye on her, too.

TRAVEL SAFELY

You may be tempted to have your pet ride in your car without being confined to his cage. You may have seen pictures of birds perched on car headrests in magazines or been intrigued by the concept of an avian car seat. Please resist these temptations because your bird could easily fly out of an open car window or be injured severely in the event of an accident if he is not in a secure carrier or cage while traveling in your car.

ACCOMMODATIONS ON THE ROAD

If you will be moving to another state, you will probably need to make hotel or motel reservations along the way. As you do, ask if the hotel or motel allows pets. (The Auto Club guidebooks and other guides often provide this information, but it doesn't hurt to check the policy as you're making reservations.) Ask for no-smoking rooms if possible to keep you and your bird healthy, and be prepared to clean up after your grey at the hotel or motel, because this will make it easier for bird owners who come after you to keep their pets in their rooms.

Before you travel with your grey, take him to the veterinarian to make sure he is in top health.

As you're packing your belongings, remember to pack a cooler or ice chest for your bird. Take along an adequate supply of your bird's present food, as well as a jug or two of the water your bird is used to drinking. Your bird will be able to handle the stress of moving better if he has familiar food and water to eat and drink along the way.

HEALTH CHECK

Before you move, make a final appointment with your bird's veterinarian. Have the bird evaluated, and ask for a health certificate (this may come in handy when crossing state lines). Also ask for a copy of your grey's records that you can take with you, or arrange to have a copy sent to your new address so your bird's new avian veterinarian will know your pet's history.

Once you've settled in your new home, set up a rapport with an avian veterinarian in the area and schedule your grey for a new patient exam. That way, you'll know your bird came through the move with flying colors!

IF YOUR MOVE IS ABROAD

If you will be taking your bird abroad, you will need to do some advance preparation to assure that you and your grey will make the move easily. This means contacting the United States Department of Agriculture (USDA) and asking them for information on taking a pet bird out of the country. You should also contact the consulate or embassy of the country you will be moving to, to ensure that your grey will be welcome. Ask if a health certificate is required, and if your bird may be quarantined before entering the country. If he will be quarantined, will you as the owner be responsible for making quarantine arrangements? Be aware that finding answers to these questions may take several phone calls, or a combination of letters, faxes and phone calls, and patience is the key to success.

Keep detailed notes about what you are told, and make sure to ask for the name of the person you're speaking with. If possible, try to speak to the same person each time you call the USDA or the embassy. When you return to the states, contact the USDA again to determine what the latest rules and regulations are for bringing your grey buddy home with you!

A VACATION COMPANION?

If your grey enjoys traveling, you may be tempted to take him on a vacation with you. This decision I leave entirely in your hands, although I generally advise against people taking their pet birds along on vacations; I leave Sindbad in the care of trusted friends or her avian veterinarian's office when I'm away. I believe greys do not find travel enlightening or broadening and are better left in familiar surroundings. However, you may feel differently and may want to expose your pet to new places and people. If so, follow the advice given regarding health certificates and traveling abroad to help ensure that you and your grey make the most of your travels!

PET SITTERS

Should you choose to leave your pet at home while you're away, you have several care options available to you. First, you can recruit the services of a trusted friend or relative, which is an inexpensive and convenient solution for many pet owners. In many cases, you can return the pet-sitting favor for your friend or relative when he or she goes out of town.

A trusted friend or relative can make a wonderful companion for your grey while you're away.

If your trusted friends and relatives live far away, you can hire a professional pet sitter (many advertise in the yellow pages, and some offer additional services, such as picking up mail, watering your plants and leaving lights and/or radios on to make your home look occupied while you're gone). If you're unsure about what to look for in a pet sitter, the National Association of Pet Sitters offers the following tips.

Look for a bonded pet sitter who carries commercial liability insurance. Ask for references and for a written description of services and fees.

Arrange to have the pet sitter come to your home before you leave on your trip to meet your pet and discuss what services you would like him or her to perform while you're away. During the initial interview, evaluate the sitter. Does he or she seem comfortable with your bird? Does the sitter have experience caring for birds? Does he or she own birds?

Ask for a written contract and discuss the availability of vet care (does he or she have an existing arrangement with your veterinarian, for example) and what arrangements the sitter makes for inclement weather or personal illness.

Discuss what the sitter's policy is for determining when a pet owner has returned home. Does he or she visit the home until the owners return? Will he or she call to ensure you've arrived home safely and your pets are cared for, or will you have to call and notify the sitter?

If the prospect of leaving your bird with a pet sitter doesn't appeal to you, you may be able to board your bird at your avian vet's office. In the last case, of course, you'll need to determine if your vet's office offers boarding services and if you want to risk your bird's health by exposing him to other birds during boarding.

I have used the services of trusted friends and my avian veterinarians' offices, and have been equally pleased on both counts. In some cases, my friends were experienced bird owners, while others were simply animal lovers who enjoyed the company of my pet as much as I did. When leaving Sindbad with my avian vet, I believe she is in good hands.

chapter 4

Bringing Your
African Grey
Home

Before you bring your feathered friend home, deter-
mine where she will live in
your house or apartment.
Selecting your grey's cage
will be one of the most
important decisions you will
make for your pet, and
where that cage will be
located in your home is
equally important. Don't wait
until you bring your bird
home to think this through.
You'll want your new pet to
settle in to her surroundings
right away, rather than
adding to her stress by relo-
cating her several times
before selecting the right
spot for the cage.

Choosing a Cage

When selecting a cage for your grey, make sure the bird has room to spread her wings without touching the cage sides. Her tail should not touch the cage bottom, nor should her head brush the top. A cage that measures 2 feet by 2 feet by 3 feet is the minimum size for a single grey, and bigger is often better, although some breeders believe that the sometimes clumsy greys do better in a minimum-size cage.

Make sure that the cage you choose has room for your grey to spread her wings without touching the cage sides.

CHECK THE FINISH

Examine any cage you choose carefully before making your final selection. If you are choosing a powder-coated cage, make sure that the finish is not chipped, bubbled or peeling, because your pet may find the spot and continue removing the finish, which can cause a cage to look old and worn before its time. Also, your pet could become ill if she ingests any of the finish. If you are considering a galvanized cage, be aware that some birds can become ill from ingesting pieces of the galvanized wire. You can prevent this "new cage syndrome" by washing down the cage wires thoroughly with a solution of vinegar and water, then scrubbing the cage with a wire brush to loosen any stray bits of galvanized wire. Rinse the cage thoroughly with water and allow it to dry before putting your bird into her new home.

Reject any cages that have sharp interior wires or wide bar spacing. (Recommended bar spacing for greys is about ½ inch.) Sharp wires could poke your bird or she could become caught between bars that are slightly wider than recommended. Also be aware that some birds may injure themselves on ornate scrollwork that decorates some cages. Finally, make sure the cage you choose has some horizontal bars in it so your grey will be able to climb the cage walls easier if she wants to exercise.

Cage Door Options

Once you've checked the overall cage quality and the bar spacing, look at the cage door. Does it open easily for you, yet remain secure enough to keep your bird in her cage when you close the door? Some African greys become quite good at letting themselves out of their cages if the cage doors do not close securely. If you discover you have a feathered Houdini on your hands, a small padlock may help keep your escape artist in her place.

A well-designed cage will allow you to take food and water dishes out of the cage without allowing your bird to get out as well.

Other things to consider: Is the door wide enough for you to get your hand in and out of the cage comfortably? Will your bird's food bowl fit through it easily? What direction does the door open? Some bird owners prefer that their pets have a play porch on a door that opens drawbridge style, while others are happy with doors that open to the side.

Cage Tray Considerations

Next, look at the cage tray. Does it slide in and out of the cage easily? Remember that you will be changing the paper in this tray at least once a day for the rest of your bird's life (which could be fifty years with good care). Is the tray an odd shape or size? Will paper need to be cut into unusual shapes to fit in it, or will paper towels, newspapers or clean sheets of used computer paper fit easily into it? The easier the tray is to remove and reline, the more likely you will be to change the lining of the tray daily. Can the cage tray be replaced if it becomes damaged and unusable? Ask the pet store staff before making your purchase.

*Choose a cage
with a tray that
is easy to remove
and reline.*

While we're down here, let me briefly discuss what to put in the cage tray. I recommend clean black-and-white newsprint, paper towels or clean sheets of used computer printer paper. Sand, ground corncobs or walnut shells may be sold by your pet supply store, but I don't recommend these as cage flooring materials because they tend to make owners lazy in their cage cleaning habits. These materials tend to hide feces and discarded food quite well. This can cause a bird owner to forget to change the cage tray on the principle that if it doesn't look dirty, it must not be dirty. This line of thinking can set up a thriving, robust colony of bacteria in the bottom of your bird's cage, which can lead to a sick bird if you're not careful. Newsprint and other paper products don't hide the dirt; in fact, they seem to draw attention to it, which leads conscientious bird owners to keep their pets' homes scrupulously clean.

You may see sandpaper or "gravel paper" sold in some pet stores as a cage tray liner. This product is supposed to provide a bird with an opportunity to ingest grit, which is purported to help aid her digestion by providing coarse grinding material that will help break up food in the bird's gizzard. However, many avian experts do not believe that a pet bird needs grit, and if a bird stands on sandpaper, she could become prone to foot problems caused by the rough surface of the paper. For your pet's health, please don't use these gravel-coated papers.

You may notice that some of the cages for African greys feature cage aprons, which help keep the debris your bird will create in the course of a day off your floor and somewhat under control. Cage aprons make cleaning up after your pet quicker and easier, and they also protect your carpet or flooring from discarded food and bird droppings if your bird decides to perch on the edge of her cage.

CAGE FLOOR

Finally, check the floor of the cage you've chosen. Does it have a grille that will keep your bird out of the debris that falls to the bottom of the cage, such as feces, seed hulls, molted feathers and discarded food? To ensure your pet's long-term good health, it's best to have a grille between your curious pet and the remains of her day in the cage tray. Also, it's easier to keep your grey in her cage while you're cleaning the cage tray if there's a grille between the cage and the tray.

SUPPLIES FOR YOUR GREY

Here's what you'll need to look for at the pet store to set your grey up right!

- a cage
- food and water bowls (at least two sets of each for easier dish changing and cage cleaning)
- perches of varying diameters and materials
- a sturdy scrub brush to clean the perches
- food (a good-quality fresh seed mixture or a formulated diet, such as pellets or crumbles)
- a powdered vitamin and mineral supplement to sprinkle on your pet's fresh foods
- a variety of safe, fun toys
- a cage cover (an old sheet or towel that is free of holes and ravels will serve this purpose nicely)
- a playgym to allow your grey time out of her cage and a place to exercise

---

WHERE TO PUT THE CAGE

Now that you've picked the perfect cage for your pet, where will you put her in your home? Your grey will be happiest when she can feel like she's part of the family, so the living room, family room or dining room may be among the best places for your bird. Avoid keeping your bird in the bathroom or kitchen, though, because sudden temperature fluctuations or fumes from cleaning products used in those rooms could harm your pet. Another spot to avoid is a busy hall or entryway, because the activity level in these spots may be too much for your pet.

Set up the cage so that it is at your eye level if possible, because it will make servicing the cage and visiting with your pet easier for you. It will also reduce the stress on your grey, because birds like to be up high for security. Also, they do not like to have people or things looming over them, so consider items such as ceiling fans, chandeliers or swag lamps. If members of your family are particularly tall, they may want to sit next to the cage or crouch down slightly to talk to the grey.

Whatever room you select, be sure to put the cage in a secure corner (with one solid wall behind the cage to ensure your grey's sense of security) and near a window. Please don't put the cage in direct sun, though, because greys can quickly overheat.

Additional Supplies

Along with the perfect-sized cage in the ideal location in your home, your pet will need a few cage accessories. These include food and water dishes, perches, toys and a cage cover.

FOOD AND WATER DISHES

Greys seem to enjoy food crocks, which are open ceramic bowls that allow them to hop up on the edge of the bowl and pick and choose what they will eat during the day. Crocks are also heavy enough to prevent mischievous birds from upending their food bowls, which can leave the bird hungry and the owner with quite a mess to clean up. You may also want to consider purchasing a cage with locking bowl holders, because bowls that are locked in place (but are still easy to remove by bird owners at mealtime) are less likely to be tipped over by your grey.

If your grey isn't prone to tipping over bowls, she may do well with a clean plastic tray from frozen dinners or a metal pie plate. Be sure to purchase shallow dishes that are less than 1 inch deep to ensure that your bird has easy access to her food at all times. When purchas-ing dishes for your grey, pick up several sets so that mealtime cleanups are quick and easy.

Most greys like to snack out of food crocks because they are easy to hop up on.

PERCHES

When choosing perches for your pet's cage, try to buy two different diame-ters or materials so your bird's feet won't get tired of standing on the same-sized perch of the same material day after day. Think of how tired your feet would feel if you stood on a piece of wood in your bare feet all day, then imagine how it would feel to stand on that piece of wood bare-foot every day for years. Sounds pretty uncomfortable, doesn't it? That's basically what your bird has to look forward to if you don't vary her perching choices.

The recommended diameter for African grey perches is 1 inch, so try to buy one perch that's this size and one that is slightly larger (1½ inches, for example) to give your pet a chance to stretch her foot muscles. Birds spend almost all of their lives standing, so keep-ing their feet healthy is important. Also, avian foot problems are much easier to prevent than they are to treat.

You'll probably notice a lot of different kinds of perches when you visit your pet store. Along with the traditional wooden dowels, bird owners can now

43

purchase perches made from manzanita branches, PVC tubes, rope, terra-cotta or concrete.

Manzanita offers birds varied diameters on the same perch, along with chewing possibilities, while PVC is pretty indestructible. (Make sure any PVC perches you offer your bird have been scuffed slightly with sandpaper to improve traction on the perch.) Rope perches also offer varied diameter and a softer perching surface than wood or plastic, and terra-cotta and concrete provide slightly abrasive surfaces that birds can use to groom their beaks without severely damaging the skin on their feet in the process.

Varying the texture and size of your grey's perches will keep her feet healthy.

Some bird owners have reported that their pets have suffered foot abrasions with these perches, however; watch your pet carefully for signs of sore feet (an inability to perch or climb, favoring a foot or raw, sore skin on the feet) if you choose to use these perches in your pet's cage. If your bird shows signs of lameness, remove the abrasive perches immediately and arrange for your avian veterinarian to examine your bird.

To further help your bird avoid foot problems, do not use sandpaper covers on her perches. These sleeves, touted as nail-trimming devices, really do little to trim a parrot's nails because birds don't usually drag their nails along their perches. What the sandpaper perch covers are good at doing, though, is abrading the surface of your grey's feet, which can leave them vulnerable to infections and can make moving about the cage painful for your pet.

When placing perches in your bird's cage, try to vary the heights slightly so your bird has different "levels" in her cage. Don't place any perches over food or water dishes, because birds can and will contaminate food or water by defecating in it. Finally, place one perch higher than the rest for a nighttime sleeping roost. Greys and other parrots like to sleep on the highest point they can find to perch, so please provide this security for your pet.

THE CAGE COVER

One important, but sometimes overlooked, accessory is the cage cover. Be sure that you have something to cover your grey's cage with when it's time to put your pet to sleep each night. The act of covering the cage seems to calm many pet birds and convince them that it's really time to go to bed although they may hear the sounds of an active family evening in the background. You may also want to cover your grey's cage during the day to calm her if she becomes frightened or to quiet her if she should burst into loud vocalizations. I cover Sindbad's cage when she becomes too vocal in order to keep peace with my neighbors, whose living room is on the other side of one of the common walls in my townhouse. You certainly don't want African greys to get a bad retutation! Another benefit of the cage cover is that it can help protect your bird from drafts.

You can purchase a cage cover, or your can use an old sheet, blanket or towel that is clean and free of holes. Be aware that some birds like to chew on their cage covers through the cage bars. If your bird does this, replace the cover when it becomes too worn to do its job effectively. Replacing a well-chewed cover will also help keep your bird from becoming entangled in the cover or caught in a ragged clump of threads. Some birds have injured themselves quite severely by being caught in a worn cage cover, so help keep your pet safe from this hazard.

Entertaining Your Grey

Your new pet has an active, agile mind that needs regular stimulation and challenges. A bored bird is often a destructive, noisy bird and doesn't make an ideal pet to boot.

Greys thrive on an active and stimulating environment.

Along with her toys, I offer Sindbad what I consider to be an interesting variety of food, both in the morning and in the evening. In addition to its nutritional value, I hope that she finds mealtime more enjoyable and somewhat mentally stimulating as a result.

When I am at work, I leave a radio on for Sindbad. Initially, I hoped that she would learn a clever jingle or two during the day, but now I give her some background noise so that her environment doesn't become too quiet, which can be stressful for some birds.

When I'm home, Sindbad wants to be part of whatever I'm doing. She joins me on the couch to cuddle, watch TV and have her head scratched, or she sits on my desk while I write, providing both inspiration and diversion.

CHOOSING THE RIGHT TOYS

Toys for an African grey can be as complex as you care to purchase or as simple as an empty paper towel roll. Depending on her mood, Sindbad can be captivated by an intricate toy with many pieces of wood strung together on knotted leather thongs, or she can be entertained by daintily nibbling on subscription cards torn out of magazines. She also seems to favor brightly colored toys with little parrot cookies on them, along with toys that have a great number of knots on them. On the average, she has four toys in her cage, and I rotate them about twice a month.

Introducing New Toys

When I introduce a brand-new toy to Sindbad, I set it next to her cage for about a week before I put it in her cage so she can become accustomed to it. If I detect any signs of fear, such as shaking, panting or feather fluffing to make herself look larger, I put the toy away for a few weeks, then reintroduce it. More familiar toys, such as an exact replacement for one that she has recently destroyed, can be added to her cage almost immediately.

Size

First, is the toy the right size for your bird? Large toys can be intimidating to small birds, which makes the birds less likely to play with them. On the other end of the spectrum, larger parrots can easily destroy toys designed for smaller birds, and they can sometimes injure themselves severely in the process.

Safety First

Next, is the toy safe? Good choices include sturdy wooden toys (either undyed or painted with bird-safe vegetable dye or food coloring) strung on closed-link chains or vegetable-tanned leather thongs, and rope toys. If you purchase rope toys for your grey, make sure her nails are trimmed regularly to prevent them from snagging in the rope and discard the toy when it becomes frayed to prevent accidents from happening.

Unsafe items to watch out for are brittle plastic toys that can be shattered easily by a grey's beak, lead-weighted toys that can be cracked open to expose the dangerous lead to curious birds, loose link chains that can catch toenails or beaks, or jingle-type bells that can trap toes, tongues or beaks.

Some entertaining toys can be made at home. Give your bird an empty paper towel roll or toilet paper tube (from unscented paper only, please), string some Cheerios on a piece of vegetable-tanned leather or offer your bird a dish of raw pasta pieces to destroy.

GAMES

Along with toys, you can play games with your African grey to amuse her and yourself. Here are some examples:

The "shell game" A variation from the carnival sideshow. In the avian version, you can hide a favorite treat under a nut cup or paper muffin cup and let your bird guess which shell hides the prize.

The great escape Offer your bird a clean, knotted-up piece of rope or vegetable-tanned leather and see how long it takes your pet to untie the knots. Give your bird extra points if she doesn't chew through any of the knots to untie them.

The mechanic Give your grey a clean nut and bolt with the nut screwed on and see how long it takes your bird to undo the nut. Make sure the nut and bolt are large enough that your pet won't swallow either accidentally while playing.

Peek-a-boo This is one of Sindbad's favorites. I put a beach towel over her, then let her work her way out from under it. She's come to expect the lavish praise I heap on her for being so clever as to find her way out every time.

Peek-a-boo! I bet you can't find me.

Tug-of-war Give your bird one end of an empty paper towel roll and tug gently. Chances are your parrot won't easily let go, or if she does, she will quickly be back for more!

In addition to playing games with you, you should encourage your grey to learn how to entertain herself from an early age so she does not become overly dependent on you, because this overdependence may lead to feather picking if the bird feels neglected. I've gotten Sindbad accustomed to playing by herself in the morning while I prepare her breakfast and in the evening before I give her her dinner. I place her atop her cage and let her play with some toys there, or I cover her gently with a towel and let her find her way out from under it. She will entertain herself for about thirty minutes, and then she's wound down enough to eat and play quietly in her cage.

The playgym is a fun way for your grey to get the exercise that she needs.

THE PLAYGYM

Although your grey will spend quite a bit of time in her cage, she will also need time out of her cage to exercise and to enjoy a change of scenery. A playgym can help keep your pet physically and mentally active.

If you visit a large pet store or bird specialty store, or if you look through the pages of any pet bird hobbyist magazine, you will see a variety of playgyms on display. You can choose a complicated gym with a series of ladders, swings, perches and toys, or you can purchase a simple T-stand that has a place for food and water bowls and an eye-screw or two from which you can hang toys. If you're really handy with tools, you can even construct a gym to your grey's specifications. The choice is up to you.

As with the cage, location of your grey's playgym will be a consideration. You will want to place the gym in a secure location in your home that is safe from other curious pets, ceiling fans, open windows and other household hazards. You will also want the gym to be in a spot frequented by your family, so your bird will have company while she plays and supervision so she doesn't get herself into trouble.

Consider placing the playgym by a window or in a spot where your bird can watch TV. She can gain additional entertainment by watching wild birds outside or whatever you're watching on TV while she's out for exercise. Think how dull your workout on the treadmill at the gym can be if you forget your tape player—your bird may need some additional visual excitement while she's working out, too!

chapter 5

Feeding Your African Grey

When Sindbad came to me, she ate a fairly limited diet: sunflower seeds, fresh corn, carrots (but only if they were cut into little triangles), grapes, bananas, walnuts and peanuts. She was touted to be a fussy eater by her previous owners, so I anticipated quite a challenge as I tried to convert her to a more healthful regimen.

Sindbad's Healthy Diet

In looking over the diary I kept on Sindbad's early days with me, though, I failed to note any opposition she had to my attempts to feed her. Armed with

a copy of *The Bird Owner's Home Health and Care Handbook* by Gary Gallerstein, DVM, I set out to feed my pet a better diet than she had been eating.

Through trial and error, this is what I came up with for her: In the morning, twelve parrot Nutriberries supplemented with about a half-dozen sugar snap pea pods split to reveal the peas inside, a slice of papaya, three almonds, five or six whole baby carrots, a chunk of zucchini sliced either crosswise or into quarters and a quarter of a green apple that has been peeled and cored. She also receives twelve Nutriberries in the evening, along with a couple of almonds, another apple quarter and whatever fruits or vegetables strike her fancy at the moment.

A well-balanced, nutritious diet is recommended for all birds.

This diet is further supplemented throughout the year with bananas, pomegranates, fresh or dried peppers, broccoli, sourdough bread slices, green beans, unsweetened dry cereal, unsalted pretzels, cheddar cheese slices, vanilla wafers, graham crackers or plain animal crackers (these last "sweet" items are offered as only occasional treats, rather than regular menu items). The running joke with my friends is that the bird eats far better than I do, and I must admit her groceries take up two shelves in the refrigerator.

African grey parrots can live to be fifty years of age, but many pet birds do not live past age fifteen. When most pet grey parrots were wild-caught imported birds, it was unusual for them to live past the age of ten. Poor diet probably played a part in the significantly shortened lives of these birds. Poor diet also causes a number of health problems, including respiratory infections, poor feather condition, flaky skin and reproductive problems.

Vitamins and Minerals

According to avian veterinarian Gary Gallerstein, birds require about a dozen vitamins—A, D, E, K, B_1, B_2, niacin, B_6, B_{12}, pantothenic acid, biotin, folic acid and choline—to stay healthy, but they can only partially manufacture D_3 and niacin. A balanced diet can help provide the rest.

Along with the vitamins listed above, pet birds need trace amounts of some minerals to maintain good health. These minerals are calcium, phosphorus, sodium, chlorine, potassium, magnesium, iron, zinc, copper, sulfur, iodine and manganese. These can be provided with a well-balanced diet and a supplemental mineral block or cuttlebone.

You may be concerned if your bird is receiving adequate amounts of vitamins and minerals in his diet. If your grey's diet is mostly seeds and fresh foods, you may want to sprinkle a good-quality vitamin-and-mineral powder onto the fresh foods, where it has the best chance of sticking to the food and being eaten. Vitamin-enriched seed diets may provide some supplementation, but some of them add the vitamins and minerals to the seed hull, which your pet will discard while he's eating. Avoid adding vitamin and mineral supplements to your bird's water dish, because they can act as a growth medium for bacteria. They may also cause the water to taste different to your bird, which may discourage him from drinking.

Seeds and Grains

Ideally, your grey's diet should contain about equal parts of seed, grain and legumes, and dark green or dark orange vegetables and fruits. You can supplement these with small amounts of well-cooked meat or eggs, or dairy products. Let's look at each part of this diet in a little more detail.

First, the seeds, grain and legumes portion of your bird's diet can include clean, fresh seed from your local pet supply store. Try to buy your birdseed from a store where stock turns over quickly. The dusty box on the bottom shelf of a store with little traffic isn't as nutritious for your pet as a bulk purchase of seeds from a freshly filled bin in a busy shop. When you bring the seeds home, refrigerate them to keep them from becoming infested with seed moths.

To ensure your bird is receiving the proper nutrients from his diet, you need to know if the seed you're serving is fresh. One way to do this is to try sprouting some of the seeds. (Sprouted seeds can also tempt a finicky eater to broaden his diet.)

SPROUTING

To sprout seeds, you will need to soak them overnight in luke-warm water. Drain the water off and let the seeds sit in a closed cupboard or other out-of-the-way place for twenty-four hours. Rinse the sprouted seeds thoroughly before offering them to your bird. If the seeds don't sprout in two or three days, they aren't fresh, and you'll need to find another source for your bird's food.

Be sure, too, that your pet has an adequate supply of seeds in his dish at all times. Rather than just looking in the dish while it's in the cage, I suggest that you take the dish out and inspect it over the trash can so you can empty the seed hulls and refill the dish easily. Other items in this group that you can offer your pet include unsweetened breakfast cereals, whole-wheat bread, cooked beans, cooked rice and pasta.

FRUITS AND VEGETABLES

Dark green or dark orange vegetables and fruits contain vitamin A, which is an important part of a bird's diet and which is missing from the seeds, grains and legumes group. This vitamin helps fight off infection and keeps a bird's eyes, mouth and respiratory system healthy. Some vitamin-A–rich foods are carrots, yams, sweet potatoes, broccoli, dried red peppers and dandelion greens.

You may be wondering whether or not to offer frozen or canned vegetables and fruits to your bird. Some birds will eat frozen vegetables and fruits, while others turn their beaks up at the somewhat mushy texture of these foodstuffs. The high sodium content in some canned foods may make them unhealthy for your grey.

Frozen and canned foods will serve your bird's needs in an emergency, but I would offer only fresh foods on a regular basis.

To ensure that your grey has enough seeds, frequently inspect his dish and empty it of seed hulls.

PROTEIN

Along with small portions of the well-cooked meat I mentioned earlier, you can also offer your bird bits of tofu, water-packed tuna, fully scrambled eggs, cottage cheese, unsweetened yogurt or low-fat cheese. Don't overdo the dairy products, though, because a bird's digestive system lacks the enzyme lactase, which means it is unable to fully process dairy foods.

HEALTHFUL PEOPLE FOOD

Introduce young greys to healthful people food early so that they learn to appreciate a varied diet. Some adult birds cling tenaciously to seed-only diets, which aren't as healthy for them in the long term. Offer adult birds fresh foods, too, in the hope that they may try something new.

Whatever healthy fresh foods you offer your pet, be sure to remove food from the cage promptly to prevent spoilage and to help keep your bird healthy. Ideally, you should change the food in your bird's cage every two to four hours (about every thirty minutes in warm weather), so a grey should be all right with a tray of food to pick through in the morning, another to select from during the afternoon and a third fresh salad to nibble on for dinner.

While sharing healthy people food with your bird is completely acceptable, sharing something that you've already taken a bite of is not. Human saliva has bacteria in it that are perfectly normal for people but that are potentially toxic to birds, so please don't share partially eaten food with your pet. For your bird's health and your peace of mind, get him his own portion or plate.

Try offering grey-sized portions of nutritious food to your pet.

By the same token, please don't kiss your grey on the beak (kiss him on top of his head instead) or allow your bird to put his head into your mouth, nibble on your lips or preen your teeth. Although you may see birds doing this on television or in pictures in a magazine and think that it's a cute trick, it's really unsafe for your bird's health and well-being.

WATER

Along with providing fresh foodstuffs at least twice a day, you will need to provide your grey with fresh, clean water twice a day to maintain his good health. You may want to provide your bird water in a shallow dish, or you may find that a water bottle does the trick. If you are considering a water bottle, be aware that some clever greys have been known to stuff a seed into the drinking tube, which allows all the water to drain out of the bottle. This creates a thirsty bird and a soggy cage, neither of which are ideal situations.

Foods to Stay Away From

Now that we've looked at foods that are good for your bird, let's look briefly at those that aren't healthy for your pet. Among those foods considered harmful to pet birds are alcohol, rhubarb, avocado (the skin and the area around the pit can be toxic), as well as highly salted, sweetened or fatty foods. You should especially avoid chocolate because it contains a chemical, theobromine, which birds cannot digest as completely as people can. Chocolate can kill your grey, so resist the temptation to share this snack with your pet. You will also want to avoid giving your bird seeds or pits from apples, apricots, cherries, peaches, pears and plums, because they can be harmful to your pet's health.

Provide your greys with fresh, clean water twice a day to maintain their health.

Let common sense be your guide in choosing what foods can be offered to your bird: If it's healthy for you, it's probably okay to share. However, remember to reduce the size of the portion you offer to your bird— a smaller grey-sized portion will be more appealing to your pet than a larger, human-sized portion.

The Pelleted Diet Option

Pelleted diets are created by mixing as many as forty different nutrients into a mash and then forcing the hot mixture through a machine to form various shapes. Some pelleted diets have colors and flavors added, while others are fairly plain. These formulated diets provide more balanced nutrition for your pet bird in an easy-to-serve form that reduces the amount of wasted food and eliminates the chance for a bird to pick through a smorgasbord of healthy foods to find his favorites and reject the foods he isn't particularly fond of. Some greys accept pelleted diets quickly, while others require some persuading.

To convert your pet to a pelleted diet, offer pellets alongside of or mixed in with his current diet. Once you see that your bird is eating the pellets, begin to gradually increase the amount of pellets you offer at mealtime while decreasing the amount of other food you serve. Within a couple of weeks, your bird should be eating his pellets with gusto!

If your grey seems a bit finicky about trying pellets, another bird in the house may show your grey how yummy pellets can be, or you may have to act as if you are enjoying the pellets as a snack in front of your pet. Really play up your apparent enjoyment of this new food because it will pique your bird's curiosity and make the pellets exceedingly interesting to your pet.

Whatever you do, don't starve your bird into trying a new food. Offer new foods along with familiar favorites. This will ensure that your bird is eating and will also encourage him to try new foods. Don't be discouraged if your grey doesn't dive right in to a new food. Be patient, keep offering new foods to your bird and praise him enthusiastically when he samples something new!

FUN WITH FRUITS AND VEGETABLES

The key to a healthful diet is variety. Try giving some of the following fruits and vegetables to your grey. Don't be surprised if it takes a couple of times for him to try a new food.

Damp broccoli florets

Apple slices

Carrots

Yams

Dried red peppers

Dandelion greens

Spinach

Cantaloupe chunks

Pear slices

chapter 6

Grooming
Your
African Grey

Your grey has several grooming needs. First, she should be able to bathe regularly, and she will need to have her nails and flight feathers trimmed periodically to ensure her safety.

Although you might think that your grey's beak also needs trimming, I would argue that a healthy bird supplied with enough chew toys seems to do a remarkable job of keeping her beak trimmed. If your bird's beak becomes overgrown, though, please consult your avian veterinarian. A parrot's beak contains a

surprising number of blood vessels, so beak trimming is best left to the experts. Also, a suddenly overgrown beak may indicate that your bird is suffering from liver damage, a virus or scaly mites, all of which require veterinary care.

Bathing Your Grey

Although your grey needs to bathe, do not be surprised if she does not readily accept bathing. After sixteen years of baths in two homes, Sindbad barely tolerates them. She prefers a quick dunk under the faucet to being misted with a spray bottle and only puts up with getting wct, I believe, because she truly enjoys the sound and the feeling of the blow dryer drying her feathers.

A healthy bird with lots of chew toys is unlikely to need a beak trim. If you think that your grey does, consult your veterinarian.

You'll have to test your grey on the question of baths. Some relish them, others sneak them in by rolling in damp greens in their food bowls, while still others can hardly stand them. If you find that your bird likes to bathe, be sure to set bath time early enough in the day so your pet's feathers can dry before bedtime, or you can employ a blow dryer set on low (as I do) to help the process along.

Unless your grey has gotten herself into oil, paint, wax or some other substance that elbow grease alone won't remove and that could harm her feathers, she will not require soap as part of her bath. Under routine conditions, soaps and detergents can damage a bird's feathers by removing beneficial oils, so hold the shampoo during your grey's normal clean-up routine!

ABOUT MITE PROTECTORS

While we're discussing grooming and feather care, please don't purchase mite protectors that hang on a bird's cage or conditioning products that are applied directly to a bird's feathers. Well-cared-for greys don't have mites and shouldn't be in danger of contracting them. (If your pet does have mites, veterinary care is the most effective treatment method.) Also, the fumes from some of these products are quite strong and can be harmful to your pet's health.

Conditioners, anti-picking products and other substances that are applied to your bird's feathers will serve one purpose: to get your bird to preen herself so thoroughly that she could remove all her feathers in a particular area. If you want to encourage your bird to preen regularly and help condition her feathers, simply mist the bird regularly with clean warm water or hold her under a gentle stream from a kitchen or bathroom faucet. Your bird will take care of the rest.

Nail Trimming

Greys need their nails clipped occasionally to prevent the nails from catching on toys or perches and injuring the bird. You will need to remove only tiny portions of the nail to keep your grey's claws trimmed. Generally, a good guideline to follow is to only remove the hook on each nail, and to do this in the smallest increments possible.

You may have an easier time using a file to trim your grey's nails than a clipper.

You may find that you have better luck filing your bird's nails with an emery board than with conventional nail clippers. Whatever method you choose to use, stop trimming well before you reach the quick,

61

which is difficult to see beforehand in a grey's black toenails. If you do happen to cut the nail short enough to make it bleed, apply cornstarch or flour, followed by direct pressure, to stop the bleeding.

Wing Trimming

The goal of a properly done wing trim is to prevent your pet from flying away or flying into a window, mirror or wall while she's out of her cage. An added benefit of trimming your pet's wings is that her inability to fly well will make her more dependent on you for transportation, which should make her more manageable. However, the bird still needs enough wing feathers so that she can glide safely to the ground if she is startled and takes flight from her cage top or playgym.

Because this is a delicate balance, you may want to enlist the help of your avian veterinarian, at least the first time. Wing trimming is a task that must be performed carefully to avoid injuring your pet, so take your time if you're doing it yourself. Please *do not* just take up the largest pair of kitchen shears you own and start snipping away, because I have heard stories from avian veterinarians about birds whose owners cut off their birds' wing tips (down to the bone) in this manner.

The first step in wing feather trimming is to assemble all the things you will need and find a quiet, well-lit place to groom your pet before you catch and trim her. Your grooming tools will include

- a well-worn towel to wrap your bird in
- small, sharp scissors to do the actual trimming
- needle-nosed pliers (to pull any blood feathers you may cut accidentally)
- flour or cornstarch to act as styptic powder in case a blood feather is cut

I encourage you to groom your pet in a quiet, well-lit place because grooming excites some birds and causes them to become wiggly. Having good light to work under will make your job easier, and having a quiet work area may just calm down your pet and make her a bit more manageable.

Once you've assembled your supplies, drape the towel over your hand and catch your bird with your toweled hand. Grab your bird by the back of her head and neck, and wrap her in the towel. Hold your bird's head securely with your thumb and index finger. (Having the bird's head covered by the towel will calm her and will give her something to chew on while you clip her wings.)

Lay the bird on her back, being careful not to constrict or compress her chest (remember, birds have no diaphragms to help them breathe), and spread her wing out carefully to look for blood feathers that are still growing in. These can be identified by their waxy, tight look and their dark centers or quills, which are caused by the blood supply to the new feather.

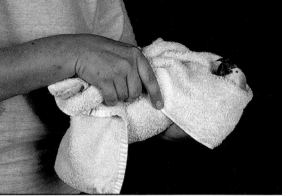

If your bird has a number of blood feathers, you may want to put off trimming her wings for a few days, because fully grown feathers cushion those just coming in from life's hard knocks. If your bird has only one or two blood feathers, you can trim the rest accordingly.

"Toweling" your grey will help you to safely groom her.

To trim your bird's feathers, separate each one away from the other flight feathers and cut it individually (remember, the goal is to have a well-trimmed bird that's still able to glide a bit if she needs to). Use the primary coverts (the set of feathers above the primary flight feathers on your bird's wing) as a guideline as to how short you can trim.

Cut the first six to eight flight feathers starting from the tip of wing, and be sure to trim an equal number of feathers from each wing. Although some people think that a bird needs only one trimmed wing, this is

*Cut the first six to
eight flight feath-
ers, and remember
to trim an equal
number of feathers
from each wing.*

incorrect and could actually cause harm to a bird that tries to fly with one trimmed and one untrimmed wing.

If you do happen to cut a blood feather, remain calm. You must remove it and stop the bleeding, and panicking will do neither you nor your bird much good.

To remove a blood feather, take a pair of needle-nosed pliers and grasp the broken feather's shaft as close to the skin of your bird's wing as you can. With one steady motion, pull the feather out completely. After you've removed the feather, put a pinch of flour or cornstarch on the feather follicle (the spot you pulled the feather out of) and apply direct pressure for a few minutes until the bleeding stops. If the bleeding doesn't stop

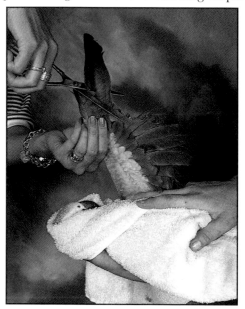

after a few minutes of direct pressure, or if you can't remove the feather shaft, contact your avian veterinarian for further instructions.

Although it may seem like you're hurting your grey by removing the broken blood feather, consider this: A broken blood feather is like an open faucet. If the feather stays in, the faucet remains open and lets the blood out. Once removed, the bird's skin generally closes up behind the feather shaft and shuts off the faucet.

Now that you've successfully trimmed your bird's wing feathers, congratulate yourself. You've just taken a great step toward keeping your bird safe. But don't rest on your laurels just yet; you must remember to check your bird's wing feathers and retrim them periodically (about four times a year as a minimum).

Be particularly alert after a molt, because your bird will have a whole new crop of flight feathers that need attention. You'll be able to tell when your bird is due for a trim when she starts becoming bolder in her flying attempts. Right after a wing trim, a grey generally tries to fly and finds she's unsuccessful at the attempt. She will keep trying, though, and may surprise you one day with a fairly good glide across her cage or off her playgym. If this happens, get the scissors and trim those wings immediately.

MOLTING

At least once a year, your grey will lose her feathers. Don't be alarmed, because this is a normal process called molting. Many pet birds seem to be in a perpetual molt, with feathers falling out and coming in throughout the summer.

Keeping your grey's wings trimmed will help prevent her from flying away.

You can consider your bird in molting season when you see a lot of whole feathers in the bottom of the cage and you notice that your bird seems to have broken out in a rash of stubby little aglets (those plastic tips on the ends of your shoelaces). These are the feather sheaths that help new pinfeathers break through the skin, and they are made of keratin (the same material that makes up our fingernails). The sheaths also help protect growing feathers from damage until the feather completes its growth cycle.

You may notice that your grey is a little more irritable during the molt; this is to be expected. Think about how you would feel if you had all these itchy new feathers coming in all of a sudden. However, your bird may actively seek out more time with you during the molt because owners are handy to have around when a grey has an itch on the top of her head that she can't quite scratch! (Scratch these new feathers gently because some of them may still be growing in and may be sensitive to the touch.)

If Your Bird Flies Away

One of the most common accidents that befalls bird owners is that a fully flighted bird escapes through an open door or window. Just because your bird has never flown before or shown any interest in leaving her cage doesn't mean that she can't fly or that she won't become disoriented once she's outside. If you don't believe it can happen, just check the lost-and-found advertisements in your local newspaper for a week. Chances are many birds will turn up in the lost column, but few are ever found.

Keep a tape recording of your grey's voice in case you need it to lure her home.

Why do lost birds never come home? Some birds fall victim to predatory animals in the wild, while others join flocks of feral, or wild, parrots (Florida and California are particularly noted for wild parrot flocks). Still other lost birds end up so far away from home because they fly wildly and frantically in any direction. And the people who find them don't advertise in the same area that the birds were lost in. Finally, some people who find lost birds don't advertise that they've been found because the finders think that whoever was unlucky or uncaring enough to lose the bird in the first place doesn't deserve to have her back.

How can you prevent your bird from becoming lost? First, make sure her wings are safely trimmed at regular intervals. Be sure to trim both wings evenly and remember to trim wings after your bird has molted.

Next, be sure your bird's cage door locks securely and that her cage tray cannot come loose if the cage is knocked over or dropped accidentally. Also be sure that all your window screens fit securely and are free from tears and large holes. Keep all window screens and patio doors closed when your bird is at liberty. Finally, don't ever go outside with your bird on your shoulder.

If, despite your best efforts, your bird should escape, you must act quickly for the best chance of recovering your pet. Here are some things to keep in mind:

- If possible, keep the bird in sight. This will make chasing her easier.

- Have an audiotape of your bird's voice and a portable tape recorder available to lure your bird back home.

- Place your bird's cage in an area where your bird is likely to see it, such as on a deck or patio. Put lots of treats and food on the floor of the cage to tempt your pet back into her home.

- Use another caged bird to attract your grey's attention.

- Alert your avian veterinarian's office that your bird has escaped. Also let the local humane society and other veterinary offices in your area know.

- Post fliers in your neighborhood describing your bird. Offer a reward and include your phone number.

- Don't give up hope.

PREVENTING BIRD THEFT

Although you may want to show off your African grey and share your bird's antics with almost complete strangers, it may not be wise to do so. Pet birds are fairly easy to steal, and African greys can command top dollar in the pet trade because of their talking ability.

So how can a pet bird owner protect his or her parrot from being stolen? Here are a few suggestions:

- Never leave your bird unattended when she's outside.

- Consider having your bird permanently identified with a microchip. This chip, which is about the size of a large grain of rice, contains a unique number that identifies your bird. The chips can be read with special scanners that are becoming more common in humane societies and animal hospitals, and bird and owner can be reunited. You can also have a sample of your bird's DNA collected and stored as a genetic fingerprint for future identification.

- If you don't want to microchip your bird, at least take clear photographs of your pet bird. If she does tricks, make a videotape of her routine. If the bird is stolen, these photographic records can make it easier for law enforcement officials to get your bird back to you.

- Don't brag to strangers about your bird. Don't record one of your bird's clever sayings on your answering machine or allow her to ride on your shoulder when you answer the door.

- If you have many birds in your home, consider installing a home security system. Install signs in your front yard and on your windows advertising this fact.

- If you will sell birds from your home, be careful what parts of your aviary you show to prospective buyers. Be suspicious if a prospective buyer focuses too much on the price of any birds for sale.

Your
African Grey's
Health

Avian Anatomy

Although you may think your
body has little in common
with your African grey's, you'd
be wrong. You both have skin,
skeletons, respiratory, cardiovascular, digestive, excretory and
nervous systems and sensory
organs, although the various systems function in slightly different ways.

SKIN

Your grey's skin is probably
pretty difficult to see since your
pet has so many feathers. If you
part the feathers carefully,
though, you can see your pet's

thin, seemingly transparent skin and the muscles beneath it. Modified skin cells help make up your bird's beak, cere, claws and the scales on his feet and legs.

SKELETAL SYSTEM

Next, let's look at your bird's skeleton. Did you know that some bird bones are hollow? They are, which makes them lighter and flying easier, but it also means that these bones may be more susceptible to breakage. For this reason, you must always handle your bird carefully! Another adaptation for flight is that the bones of a bird's wing (which correspond to our arm and hand bones) are fused for greater strength.

Birds also have air sacs in some of their bones (these are called pneumatic bones) and throughout their bodies; these air sacs help lighten the bird's body and also cool him more efficiently. Birds cannot perspire as mammals do because birds have no sweat glands, so they must have a way to cool themselves off.

Parrots have ten neck vertebrae to a human's seven. This makes a parrot's neck more free moving than a person's (a parrot can turn his head almost 180 degrees), which can be an advantage in spotting food or predators in the wild.

During breeding season, a female bird's bones become denser as they store calcium needed to create eggshells. A female's skeleton can weigh up to twenty percent more during breeding season than it does the rest of the year because of this calcium storage.

RESPIRATORY SYSTEM

Your bird's respiratory system is a highly efficient system that works in a markedly different way from yours. Here's how your bird breathes: Air enters the system through your bird's nares, passes through his sinuses and into his throat. As it does, the air is filtered through the **choana,** which is a slit that can be easily seen in the roof of many birds' mouths. The choana also helps to clean and warm the air before it goes further into the respiratory system.

After the air passes the choana, it flows through the larynx and trachea, past the **syrinx** or "voice box." Your bird doesn't have vocal cords like you do; rather, vibrations of the syrinx membrane are what allow our birds to make sounds.

So far it sounds similar to the way we breathe, doesn't it? Well, here's where the differences begin. As the air continues its journey past the syrinx and into the bronchi, your bird's **lungs** don't expand and contract to bring the air in. This is partly due to the fact that birds don't have diaphragms like people do. Instead, the bird's body wall expands and contracts, much like a fireplace bellows. This action brings air into the air sacs I mentioned earlier as part of the skeleton. This bellows action also moves air in and out of the lungs.

Although a bird's respiratory system is extremely efficient at exchanging gases in the system, two complete breaths are required to do the same work that a single breath does in humans and other mammals. This is why you may notice that your bird seems to be breathing quite quickly.

CARDIOVASCULAR SYSTEM

Along with the respiratory system, your bird's cardiovascular system keeps oxygen and other nutrients moving throughout your pet's body, although the circulatory path in your grey differs from yours. In your pet bird, blood flowing from the legs, reproductive system and lower intestines passes through the kidneys on its way back to the general circulatory system.

Like you, though, your African grey has a four-chambered heart, with two atria and two ventricles. Unlike your average heart rate of 72 beats per minute, your grey's average heart rate is 340 to 600 beats per minute.

DIGESTIVE SYSTEM

To keep this energy-efficient machine (your bird's body) running requires fuel (or food). This is where your bird's digestive system comes in. One of the main functions of the digestive system is to provide the fuel that maintains your bird's body temperature.

A bird's body temperature is higher than a human's. The first time I bird-sat for friends, I worried about their cockatoo's seemingly hot feet. After another bird owner told me that birds have higher temperatures than people, I stopped worrying about the bird's warm feet.

Your African grey's digestive system begins with his **beak.** The size and shape of a bird's beak depends on his food-gathering needs. Compare and contrast the sharp, pointed beak of an eagle or the elongated bill of a hummingbird with the hooked beak of your parrot. Notice the underside of your bird's upper beak if you can. It has tiny ridges in it that help your grey hold and crack seeds more easily.

The underside of the grey's beak has ridges that help him crack seeds with ease.

A parrot's mouth works a little differently than a mammal's. Parrots don't have saliva to help break down and move their food around like we do. Also, their taste buds are contained in the roofs of their mouths. Because they have few taste buds, experts think that a parrot's sense of taste is poorly developed.

After the food leaves your bird's mouth, it travels down the **esophagus,** where it is moistened. The food then travels to the crop, where it is moistened further and is supplied in small increments to the bird's stomach.

After the food leaves the crop, it travels through the **proventriculus,** where digestive juices are added, to the **gizzard,** where the food is broken down into even smaller pieces. The food then travels to the **small intestine,** where nutrients are absorbed into the bloodstream. Anything that's leftover then travels through the large intestine to the cloaca, which is the common

chamber that collects wastes before they leave the
bird's body through the vent. The whole process from
mouth to vent usually takes less than an hour, which is
why you may notice that your bird leaves frequent,
small droppings in his cage.

Along with the solid waste created by the digestive system, your grey's kidneys create urine, which is then
transported through ureters to the cloaca for excre-
tion. Unlike a mammal, a bird does not have a bladder
or a urethra.

NERVOUS SYSTEM

Your African grey's nervous system is very similar to
your own. Both are made up of the brain, the spinal
cord and countless nerves throughout the body that
transmit messages to and from the brain.

Now that we've examined some of the similarities
between avian and human anatomy, let's stop and look
at some of the unusual anatomical features birds have.
The first feature I'd like to discuss is probably one of
the reasons you're attracted to birds: feathers. Birds
are the only animals that have feathers, which serve
several purposes. Feathers help birds fly, they keep
birds warm, they attract the
attention of potential mates
and they help scare away
predators.

*Besides keeping
your grey warm,
feathers help your
grey to fly, attract
potential mates
and scare away
predators.*

FEATHERS

Feathers grow from follicles
that are arranged in rows
that are known as pterylae.
A feather is a remarkably
designed creation. The base
of the feather shaft, which
fits into the bird's skin, is
called the quill. It is light
and hollow, but remarkably
tough. The upper part of the feather shaft is called the
rachis. From it branch the barbs and barbules (smaller

barbs) that make up most of the feather. The barbs and barbules have small hooks on them that enable the different parts of the feather to interlock like Velcro and form the feather's vane or web.

Birds have several different types of feathers on their bodies. **Contour feathers** are the colorful outer feathers on a bird's body and wings. Many birds have an undercoating of down feathers that help keep them warm. **Semiplume feathers** are found on a bird's beak, nares (nostrils) and eyelids.

A bird's flight feathers can be classified into one of two types. **Primary flight feathers** are the large wing feathers that push a bird forward during flight. They are also the ones that need clipping. **Secondary flight feathers** are found on the inner wing, and they help support the bird in flight. Primary and secondary wing feathers can operate independently of each other. The bird's tail feathers also assist in flight by acting as a brake and a rudder to make steering easier.

Preening is a way that greys keep their feathers groomed and in healthy condition.

To keep their feathers in good condition, healthy birds will spend a great deal of time fluffing their feathers and preening them. You may see your grey seeming to pick at the base of his tail on the top side. This is a normal behavior in which the bird removes oil from the preen gland and spreads it on his feathers. The oil also helps prevent skin infections and waterproofs the feathers.

Sometimes pet birds will develop white lines or small holes on the large feathers of their wings and tails. These lines or holes are referred to as "stress bars" or "stress lines" and result from the bird being under stress as the feathers were developing. If you notice stress bars on your grey's feathers, discuss them with your avian veterinarian.

Be prepared to tell the doctor of anything new in your grey's routine, because parrots are creatures of habit that sometimes react badly to changes in their surroundings, diet or daily activities. I find stress bars on Sindbad's feathers each time she completes a course of antibiotic treatments, and I also find stress bars on her tail feathers regularly. I attribute the stress bars in her tail to the fact that she is a rather clumsy parrot and often catches or bends her developing tail feathers in the cage bars and floor grate.

You may notice some lavender feathers on your grey parrot. Sindbad's feathers take on a lavender cast when she's wet, but other grey owners I know report that their pets have lavender feathers all the time. Don't be alarmed if you notice your bird's feathers have a slightly lavender tone to them; it's nothing to worry about. Other owners of African greys may notice that their birds have red spots on their feathers or that the birds sprout red feathers where grey ones should be. Again, don't panic.

African grey experts have a variety of causes for these unusually colored feathers, ranging from excessive beta carotene in the bird's diet to old age. Other bird experts think red feathers indicate a medical problem, such as psittacine beak and feather disease syndrome (PBFDS), liver problems, kidney dysfunction or systemic disease. In my experience, red feathers result from a feather-picking bird that finally decides to leave her feathers alone after repeatedly chewing them off and letting them grow in.

African Grey Senses
SIGHT

Although I mentioned earlier that birds have a poor sense of taste, they have a well-developed sense of sight. Birds can see detail and they can discern colors. Be aware of this when selecting cage accessories for your pet, because some birds react to a change in the color of their food dishes. Some seem excited by a different color bowl, while others act fearful of the new item. Sindbad, for example, recognizes her black food trays and her red, blue, brown or ivory water bowls, but if I offer her food or water in a different color tray or bowl, she is hesitant to eat or drink right away. She must become accustomed to the new food vessel before she eats or drinks, a process that can take as little as a few minutes or as long as half a day.

Because their eyes are located on the sides of their heads, most pet birds rely on monocular vision, which mean that they use each eye independent of the other. If a bird really wants to study an object, you will often see him tilt his head to one side and examine the object with just one eye. Birds aren't really able to move their eyes around very much, but they compensate for this by having highly mobile necks that allow them to turn their heads about 180 degrees.

Greys have monocular vision— they use each eye independent of the other.

Like cats and dogs, birds have third eyelids called nictitating membranes that you will sometimes see flick briefly across your parrot's eye. The purpose of this membrane is to keep the eyeball moist and clean. If you see your bird's nictitating membrane for more than a brief second, please contact your avian veterinarian for an evaluation. You have probably noticed that your bird lacks eyelashes. In their place are small feathers called semiplumes that help keep dirt and dust out of the bird's eyeball.

HEARING

You may be wondering where your grey's ears are. Look carefully under the feathers behind and below each eye to find them. The ears are the somewhat large holes in the sides of your parrot's head. Greys have about the same ability to distinguish sound waves and determine the location of the sound as people do, but birds seem to be less sensitive to higher and lower pitches than their owners.

TASTE AND SMELL

You may be wondering how your parrot's senses of smell and taste compare to your own. Birds seem to have poorly developed senses of smell and taste because smells often dissipate quickly in the air (where flying birds spend their time) and because birds have fewer taste buds in their mouths than people do. (Parrot taste buds are located in the roof of the birds' mouths, not in the tongue like ours are.)

TOUCH

The final sense we relate to, touch, is well-developed in parrots. Parrots use their feet and their mouths to touch their surroundings (young birds particularly seem to "mouth" everything they can get their beaks on), to play and to determine what is safe to perch on or chew on and what's good to eat.

Along with their tactile uses, a parrot's feet also have an unusual design compared to other caged birds. Look at your parrot's. Do you notice that two of your bird's toes point forward and two point backward? This two toes forward and two toes back arrangement is called zygodactyl, and it allows a parrot to hold food or toys in his foot and to climb around easily.

Visiting a Veterinarian

With good care, a grey parrot can live up to fifty years, although the average life span of a pet grey is about fifteen years. As a caring owner, you want your bird to have good care and the best chance at living a long, healthy life. To that end, you will need to locate a veterinarian who understands the special medical needs of birds with whom you can establish a good working relationship.

The best time to do this is when you first bring your bird home from the breeder or pet store. If possible, arrange to visit your veterinarian's office on your way home from the breeder or store. This is particularly important if you have other birds at home, because you don't want to endanger the health of your existing flock or your new pet.

If you don't know an avian veterinarian in your area, ask the person you bought your grey from where he or she takes his or her birds. (Breeders and bird stores usually have avian veterinarians on whom they depend.) Talk to other bird owners you know and find out who they take their pets to, or call bird clubs in your area for referrals.

If you have no bird-owning friends or can't locate a bird club, your next best bet is the yellow pages. Read the advertisements for veterinarians carefully, and try to find one who specializes in birds. Many veterinarians who have an interest in treating birds will join the Association of Avian Veterinarians and advertise themselves as members of this organization. Some veterinarians have taken and passed a special examination that entitles them to call themselves avian specialists.

Once you've received your recommendations or found likely candidates in the telephone book, start calling the veterinary offices. Ask the receptionist how many birds the doctor sees in a week or month, how much an office visit costs, and what payment options are available (cash, credit card, check or time payments). You can also inquire if the doctor keeps birds as his or her personal pets.

If you like the answers you receive from the receptionist, make an appointment for your parrot to be evaluated. (If you don't, of course, move on to the next name on your list.) Make a list of any questions you want to ask the doctor regarding diet, how often your bird's wings and nails should be clipped or how often you should bring the bird in for an examination.

Plan to arrive a little early for your first appointment because you will be asked to fill out a patient information form. This form will ask you for your bird's name, his age and sex, the length of time you have owned him, your name, address and telephone number, your preferred method of paying for veterinary services, how you heard about the veterinary office and the name and address of a friend the veterinary office can contact in case of emergency. The form may also ask you to express your opinion on the amount of money you would spend on your pet in an emergency, because this can help the doctor know what kind of treatment to recommend in such circumstances.

WHAT THE VETERINARIAN MAY ASK YOU

Bird owners should not be afraid to ask their avian veterinarians questions. Avian vets have devoted a lot of time, energy and effort to studying birds, so put this resource to use whenever you can.

What bird owners may not know is that they may be asked a number of questions by the veterinarian. When you take your bird in for an exam, be aware that the doctor may ask you for answers to these questions:

- Why is the bird here today?
- What's the bird's normal activity level like?
- How is the bird's appetite?
- What does the bird's normal diet consist of?
- Have you noticed a change in the bird's appearance lately?

Be sure to explain any changes in as much detail as you can, because changes in your bird's normal behavior can indicate illness.

During the initial examination, the veterinarian will probably take his or her first look at your parrot while he is still in his cage or carrier. The doctor may talk to you and your bird for a few minutes to give the bird an opportunity to become accustomed to him or her, rather than simply reaching right in and grabbing your pet. While the veterinarian is talking to you, he or she will check the bird's posture and his ability to perch.

Next, the doctor should remove the bird from his carrier or cage and look him over carefully. He or she will particularly note the condition of your pet's eyes, his beak and his nares (nostrils). The bird should be weighed, and the veterinarian will probably palpate (feel) your parrot's body and wings for any lumps, bumps or deformities that require further investigation. Feather condition will also be assessed, as will the condition of the bird's vent, legs and feet.

COMMON AVIAN TESTS

After your veterinarian has completed your grey's physical examination, he or she may recommend further tests. These can include:

- Blood workups to help a doctor determine if your bird has a specific disease. Blood tests can be further broken down into a complete blood count, which determines how many platelets, red and white blood cells your bird has (this information can help diagnose infections or anemia) and a blood chemistry profile, which helps a veterinarian analyze how your bird's body processes enzymes, electrolytes and other chemicals.

- Radiographs or x-rays, which allow a veterinarian to study the size and shape of a bird's internal organs, along with the formation of his bones. X-rays also help doctors find foreign bodies in a bird's system.

- Microbiological exams to help a veterinarian determine if any unusual organisms (bacteria, fungi or yeast) are growing inside your bird's body.

- Fecal analysis, a study of a small sample of your bird's droppings, to determine if he has internal parasites or a bacterial or yeast infection.

After the examination, you will have a chance to talk with your veterinarian. The doctor will probably recommend a follow-up examination schedule for your pet. Most healthy birds visit the veterinarian annually, but some have to go more frequently.

Sexing Greys

African greys are difficult to sex visually. Males essentially look like females, which can make setting up true breeding pairs impossible. Although some longtime breeders can obtain a fair degree of accuracy by observing their birds, pet owners and novice breeders shouldn't try to visually sex their birds, or you may end up like me, who had my so-called "male" bird lay eggs after being a pet for sixteen years.

If you are going to set up birds for breeding, the following sexing methods are available: observation, DNA sexing, surgical sexing, fecal analysis and feather sexing. Here are brief descriptions of these methods:

Observation is the method I finally used to determine Sindbad's gender, and it came out, "Gee, he laid an egg," when I explained what had happened to friends.

DNA sexing analyzes red blood cells to determine which chromosomes—male or female—are present. Your veterinarian takes a blood sample from your bird and sends it to a laboratory for examination. Results are available in about three weeks.

Surgical sexing requires that a small incision is made in the bird's side under anesthesia, and your veterinarian inserts an endoscope into the incision to look for either an ovary if the bird is female or a testicle if the bird is male. Although it might seem risky, surgical sexing is quite safe if performed by an experienced avian veterinarian.

Fecal analysis examines a small sample of the bird's droppings for the presence of reproductive hormones. This test is only effective with sexually mature birds.

Feather sexing looks at feather pulp from a blood feather for the presence of sex chromosomes. The feather is kept on ice and sent to a laboratory by overnight mail for evaluation.

Your avian veterinarian can further discuss these sexing methods with you and help you decide which is the best one to use on your breeder birds.

Medicating Your Grey
Most bird owners are faced with the prospect of medicating their pets at some point in the birds' lives, and

many are unsure if they can complete the task without hurting their pets. If you have to medicate your pet, your avian veterinarian or veterinary technician should explain the process to you. In the course of the explanation, you should find out how you will be administering the medication, how much of a given drug you will be giving your bird, how often the bird needs the medication and how long the entire course of treatment will last.

If you find (as I often have) that you've forgotten one or more of these steps after you arrive home with your bird and your instructions, call your vet's office for clarification to ensure that your bird receives the follow-up care from you that he needs to recover.

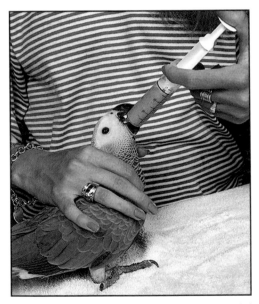

Let's briefly review the most common methods of administering medications to birds, which are discussed completely in *The Complete Bird Owner's Handbook* by Gary A. Gallerstein, DVM. They are oral, injected and topical.

ORAL MEDICATION

This is a good route to take with birds that are small, easy to handle or underweight. The medication is usually given with a needleless plastic syringe

When medicating a bird by mouth, use a needleless plastic syringe.

placed in the left side of the bird's mouth and pointed toward the right side of his throat. This route is recommended to ensure that the medication gets into the bird's digestive system and not into his lungs, where aspiration pneumonia can result.

Medicating a bird's food or offering medicated feed (such as tetracyline-laced pellets that were fed to imported birds during quarantine to prevent psittacosis) is another effective possibility, but medications added to a bird's water supply are often less effective because sick birds frequently avoid drinking water, and the medicated water may have an unusual taste that makes a bird less likely to drink it.

INJECTED MEDICATION

Avian veterinarians consider this the most effective meth-od of medicating birds. Some injection sites— into a vein, beneath the skin or into a bone—are used by avian veterinarians in the clinic setting. Bird owners are usually asked to medicate their birds intramuscularly, or by injecting medication into the bird's chest muscle. This is the area of the bird's body that has the greatest muscle mass, so it is a good injection site.

It's perfectly understandable if you're hesitant about giving your bird shots. I was the first time I had to medicate Sindbad this way, but we both survived the procedure. Wrap your bird securely, but comfortably, in a small towel, and lay him on your lap with his chest up. Hold his head securely with your thumb and index finger of one hand, and use the other to insert the syringe at about a 45° angle under the bird's chest feathers and into the muscle beneath.

You should remember to alternate the side you inject your bird on (say, left in the morning and right in the evening) to ensure that one side doesn't get overly injected and sore, and you should remain calm and talk to your bird in a soothing tone while you're administering the drugs. Before you both know it, the

---

SIGNS OF ILLNESS

To help your veterinarian and to keep your pet from suffering long-term health risks, keep a close eye on his daily activities and appearance. If something suddenly changes in the way your bird looks or acts, contact your veterinarian immediately. Birds naturally hide signs of illness to protect themselves from predators, so by the time a bird looks or acts sick, he may already be dangerously ill.

Some signs of illness include

- a fluffed-up appearance
- a loss of appetite
- sleeping all the time
- a change in the appearance or number of droppings
- weight loss
- listlessness
- drooping wings
- lameness
- partially eaten food stuck to the bird's face or food regurgitated onto the cage floor
- labored breathing, with or without tail bobbing
- runny eyes or nose
- the bird stops talking or singing

If your bird shows any of these signs, please contact your veterinarian's office immediately.

shot is over and your bird is one step closer to a complete recovery!

TOPICAL MEDICATION

This method, which is far less stressful than the one we just discussed, provides medication directly to part of a bird's body. Uses can include medications for eye infections, dry skin on the feet or legs or sinus problems.

Sindbad and I are living proof that all the methods described above work and are survivable by both bird and owner. She has received oral and injectable antibiotics for recurring infections, and she has had topical ointments applied to her feet to clear up a dry skin problem. Although I would have doubted that I would be able to give her injections when I first adopted her nine years ago, I now know that I can do it with a minimal amount of stress for both of us.

Grey Parrot Health Concerns

African grey parrots are prone to feather picking, hypocalcemia, aspergillosis, papillomas and psittacine beak and feather disease syndrome (PBFDS). Greys fed seed-only diets can also become prone to vitamin A deficiency and other nutritionally related disorders.

HYPOCALCEMIA

Hypocalcemia (low blood calcium level) is usually indicated by occasional convulsions or tremors. Other signs of calcium deficiency can include a loss of coordination, seizures, weak bones and poor egg formation. African greys seem more prone to this problem than other parrot species.

You can supply calcium to your grey by offering him calcium-rich foods, such as low-fat cheese or yogurt; by applying calcium powder (available at your pet supply store) to your pet's fresh foods; by adding a pediatric liquid calcium supplement to your bird's drinking water; or by offering mineral blocks and cuttlebones. In hypocalcemic birds, a high-calcium diet is usually only required until the bird's calcium levels are restored. Ask your avian veterinarian what type of diet is best for your grey.

The possible causes of hypocalcemia include chronic kidney or parathyroid problems, but many cases of hypocalcemia have no known cause. In young greys, hypocalcemia can result in spontaneous long bone fractures.

Feeding a balanced diet is your best defense against hypocalcemia, because seed-only diets have been implicated as a cause of the condition.

ASPERGILLOSIS

Aspergillosis is caused by a fungus, Aspergillus. It can settle in a bird's respiratory tract and cause breathing difficulties. This disease was once considered untreatable, but promise has been shown with some antifungal medications from human medicine.

PAPILLOMAS

Papillomas, which are benign tumors that can appear almost anywhere on a bird's skin, including his foot, leg, eyelid or preen gland. If a bird has a papilloma on his cloaca, the bird may appear to have a "wet raspberry" coming out of his vent. These tumors, which are caused by a virus, can appear as small, crusty lesions, or they may be raised growths that have a bumpy texture or small projections.

Many papillomas can be left untreated without harm to the bird, but some must be removed by an avian veterinarian because a bird may pick at the growth and cause it to bleed.

PSITTACINE BEAK AND FEATHER DISEASE SYNDROME (PBFDS)

Psittacine beak and feather disease syndrome (PBFDS) has been a hot topic among birdkeepers for the last decade. The virus was first detected in cockatoos and was originally thought to be a cockatoo-specific problem.

It has since been determined that more than forty species of parrots, including African greys, can contract this disease, which causes a bird's feathers to become pinched or clubbed in appearance.

Other symptoms include beak fractures and mouth ulcers. This highly contagious, fatal disease is most common in birds less than three years of age, and there is no cure at present. A vaccine is under development.

African Grey First Aid

Sometimes your pet will get himself into a situation that will require quick thinking and even quicker action on your part to help save your bird from serious injury or death. I'd like to outline some basic first aid techniques that may prove useful in these situations.

Before we get into the specific techniques, make sure you have your bird owner's first aid kit (see sidebar for information on what to include). Keep all these supplies in one place, such as a fishing tackle box. This will eliminate your having to search for some supplies in emergency situations, and the case can be taken along on trips or left for the bird-sitter if your bird isn't an adventurer.

In *The Complete Bird Owner's Handbook*, veterinarian Gary Gallerstein offers the following "don'ts" to bird owners whose birds need urgent care:

• Don't give a bird human medications or medications prescribed for another animal unless so directed by your veterinarian.

FIRST AID KIT

Assemble a bird owner's first aid kit so that you will have some basic supplies on hand before your bird needs them. Here's what to include:

• appropriate-sized towels for catching and holding your bird

• a heating pad, heat lamp or other heat source

• a pad of paper and pencil to make notes about bird's condition

• styptic powder, silver nitrate stick or cornstarch to stop bleeding (use styptic powder and silver nitrate stick on beak and nails only)

• blunt-tipped scissors

• nail clippers and nail file

• needle-nosed pliers to pull broken blood feathers

• blunt-end tweezers

• hydrogen peroxide or other disinfectant solution

• eye irrigation solution

• bandage materials such as gauze squares, masking tape (it doesn't stick to a bird's feathers like adhesive tape does) and gauze rolls

• Pedialyte or other energy supplement

• eye dropper

• syringes to irrigate wounds or feed sick birds

• penlight

- Don't give your bird medications that are suggested by a friend, a store employee or a human physician.

- Don't give a bird alcohol or laxatives.

- Don't apply any oils or ointments to your bird unless your veterinarian tells you to do so.

- Don't bathe a sick bird.

No matter what the situation, there are a few things to keep in mind when facing a medical emergency with your pet. First, keep as calm as possible because your bird is already excited enough from being injured, and you getting excited won't help your pet get well. Next, stop any bleeding, keep the bird warm and minimize handling him.

After you've stabilized your pet, call your veterinarian's office for further instructions. Tell them, "This is an emergency," and that your bird has had an accident. Describe what happened to your pet as clearly and calmly as you can. Listen carefully to the instructions you are given and follow them. Finally, transport your bird to the vet's office as quickly and safely as you can.

Here are some urgent medical situations that bird owners are likely to encounter, the reason that they are medical emergencies, the signs and symptoms your bird might show and the recommended treatments for the problem.

ANIMAL BITES

Infections can develop from bacteria on the biting animal's teeth and/or claws. Also, a bird's internal organs can be damaged by the bite. Sometimes the bite marks can be seen, but often the bird shows few, if any, signs of injury.

Call your veterinarian's office and transport the bird there immediately. Treatment for shock and antibiotics are often the course of action veterinarians take to save birds that have been bitten.

BEAK INJURY

A bird needs both his upper and lower beak (also called the upper and lower mandible) to eat and preen properly. Infections can also set in rather quickly if a beak is fractured or punctured.

An obvious symptom is that the bird is bleeding from his beak. This often occurs after the bird flies into a windowpane or mirror, or if he has a run-in with an operational ceiling fan. The bird may have also cracked or damaged his beak, and portions of the beak may be missing.

Control the bleeding. Keep your bird calm and quiet. Contact your avian veterinarian's office.

BLEEDING

A bird can withstand about a twenty percent loss of blood volume and still recover from an injury. In the event of external bleeding, you will see blood on the bird, his cage and his surroundings. In the case of internal bleeding, the bird may pass bloody droppings or bleed from his nose, mouth or vent.

For external bleeding, apply direct pressure. If the bleeding doesn't stop with direct pressure, apply a coagulant, such as styptic powder (for nails and beaks) or cornstarch (for broken feathers and skin injuries). If the bleeding stops, observe the bird for the restarting of the bleeding or for shock. Call your veterinarian's office if the bird seems weak or if he has lost a lot of blood and arrange to take the bird in for further treatment.

In the case of broken blood feathers, you may have to remove the feather shaft to stop the bleeding. To do this, grasp the feather shaft as close to the skin as you can with a pair of needle-nosed pliers and pull out the shaft with a swift, steady motion. Apply direct pressure to the skin after you remove the feather shaft.

BREATHING PROBLEMS

Respiratory problems in pet birds can be life threatening.

The bird wheezes or clicks while breathing, bobs his tail, breathes with an open mouth, has discharge from his nares or swelling around his eyes.

Keep the bird warm, place him in a bathroom with a hot shower running to help him breathe easier and call your veterinarian's office.

BURNS

Birds that are burned severely enough can go into shock and may die.

A burned bird has reddened skin and burnt or greasy feathers. The bird may also show signs of shock (see page 92 for details).

Mist burned area with cool water. Apply antibiotic cream or spray lightly. **Do not apply any oily or greasy substances,** including butter. If the bird seems to be in shock or the burn is widespread, contact your veterinarian's office for further instructions.

CONCUSSION

A concussion results from a sharp blow to the head that can cause injury to the brain. Birds sometimes suffer concussions when they fly into mirrors or windows. They will seem stunned and may go into shock.

Keep the bird warm, prevent him from hurting himself further and watch him carefully. Alert your veterinarian's office to the injury.

CLOACAL PROLAPSE

The bird's lower intestines, utcrus or cloaca is protruding from the bird's vent. The bird has pink, red, brown or black tissue protruding from his vent.

Contact your veterinarian's office for immediate followup care. Your veterinarian can usually reposition the organs.

EGG BINDING

The egg blocks the hen's excretory system and makes it impossible for her to eliminate. Also, eggs can sometimes break inside the hen, which can lead to infection.

An egg-bound hen strains to lay eggs unsuccessfully. She becomes fluffed and lethargic, sits on the floor of her cage, may be paralyzed and may have a swollen abdomen.

Keep the hen warm because this sometimes helps her pass the egg. Put her and her cage into a warm bathroom with a hot shower running to increase the humidity, which may also help her pass the egg. If your bird doesn't improve shortly (within a hour), contact your veterinarian.

EYE INJURY

Untreated eye problems may lead to blindness. Look for the following signs: swollen or pasty eyelids, discharge, cloudy eyeball, increased rubbing of eye area.

Examine the eye carefully for foreign bodies. Contact your veterinarian for more information.

FRACTURES

A fracture is an emergency because a fracture can cause a bird to go into shock. Depending on the type of fracture, infections can also set in.

Birds most often break bones in their legs, so be on the lookout for a bird that is holding one leg at an odd angle or that isn't putting weight on one leg. Sudden swelling of a leg or wing, or a droopy wing can also indicate fractures.

Confine the bird to his cage or a small carrier. Don't handle him unnecessarily. Keep him warm and contact your veterinarian.

FROSTBITE

A bird could lose toes or feet to frostbite. He could also go into shock and die as a result. The frostbitten area is very cold and dry to the touch and is pale in color.

Warm the damaged tissue up gradually in a circulating water bath. Keep your bird warm and contact your veterinarian's office for further instructions.

INHALED OR EATEN FOREIGN OBJECT

Birds can develop serious respiratory or digestive problems from foreign objects in their bodies. In the case of inhaled items, wheezing and other respiratory problems may result. In the case of consumed objects, consider whether the bird was seen playing with a small item that suddenly cannot be found.

If you suspect that your bird has inhaled or eaten something he shouldn't, contact your veterinarian's office immediately.

LEAD POISONING

Birds can die from lead poisoning. A bird with lead poisoning may act depressed or weak. He may be blind, or he may walk in circles at the bottom of his cage. He may regurgitate or pass droppings that resemble tomato juice.

Contact your avian veterinarian immediately. Lead poisoning requires a quick start to treatment, and the treatment may require several days or weeks to complete successfully.

Note: Lead poisoning is easily prevented by keeping birds away from common sources of lead in the home. These include stained glass items, leaded paint found in some older homes, fishing weights, drapery weights and parrot toys (some are weighted with lead). One item that won't cause lead poisoning are "lead" pencils (they're actually graphite).

OVERHEATING

High body temperatures can kill a bird. An overheated bird will try to make himself thin. He will hold his wings away from his body, open his mouth and roll his tongue in an attempt to cool himself. Birds don't have sweat glands, so they must try to cool their bodies by exposing as much of their skin's surface as they can to moving air.

Cool the bird off by putting him in front of a fan (make sure the blades are screened so the bird doesn't injure himself further), by spraying him with cool water or by having him stand in a bowl of cool water. Let the bird drink cool water if he can (if he can't, offer him cool water with an eyedropper) and contact your veterinarian.

POISONING

Poisons can kill a bird quickly. Poisoned birds may suddenly regurgitate, have diarrhea or bloody droppings, and have redness or burns around their mouths. They may also go into convulsions, become paralyzed or go into shock.

Put the poison out of your bird's reach. Contact your veterinarian for further instructions. Be prepared to take the poison with you to the vet's office in case he or she needs to contact a poison control center for further information.

SEIZURES

Seizures can indicate a number of serious conditions, including lead poisoning, infections, nutritional deficiency, heat stroke and epilepsy.

The bird goes into a seizure that lasts from a few seconds to a minute. Afterward, he seems dazed and may stay on the cage floor for several hours. He may also appear unsteady and won't perch.

Keep the bird from hurting himself further by removing everything you can from his cage. Cover the bird's cage with a towel and darken the room to reduce the bird's stress level. Contact your veterinarian's office for further instructions immediately.

SHOCK

Shock indicates that the bird's circulatory system cannot move the blood supply around the bird's body.

This is a serious condition that can lead to death if left untreated. Birds that are in shock may act depressed, they may breathe rapidly and they may have a fluffed appearance. If your bird displays these signs in conjunction with a recent accident, suspect shock and take appropriate action.

Keep your bird warm, cover his cage and transport him to your veterinarian's office as soon as possible.

Emergency Tips

Veterinarian Michael Murray recommends that bird owners keep the following tips in mind when facing emergency situations:

Keep the bird warm. You can do this by putting the bird in an empty aquarium with a heating pad under him, by putting a heat lamp near the bird's cage or by putting a heating pad set on low under the bird's cage in place of the cage tray. Whatever heat source you choose to use, make sure to keep a close eye on your bird so that he doesn't accidentally burn himself on the pad or lamp or that he doesn't chew on a power cord.

Put the bird in a dark, quiet room. This helps reduce the bird's stress.

Put the bird's food in locations that are easy to reach. Sick birds need to eat, but they may not be able to reach food in the normal locations in the cage. Sometimes, birds require hand-feeding to keep their calorie consumption steady.

Protect the bird from additional injury. If the convalescing bird is in a clear-sided aquarium, for example, you may want to put a towel over the glass to keep the bird from flying into it.

Household Hazards

Look at your home from your grey's point of view. What seems like home sweet home to you can be home unsafe home to your bird. As a responsible bird owner, you want to provide your pet with the best care possible, and part of that care requires that you essentially bird-proof your home. Let's take a room-by-room look at some of the potentially dangerous situations you should be aware of.

BATHROOM

This can be a grey's paradise if the bird is allowed to spend time with you as you prepare for work or for an evening out, but it can also be quite harmful to your bird's health. Your bird could fall into an uncovered toilet bowl and drown, he could hurt himself chewing on the cord of your blow dryer or he could be overcome by fumes from perfume, hair spray or cleaning products, such as bleach, air freshener or toilet bowl cleaner. The bird could also become ill if he nibbles on prescription or over-the-counter drugs in the medicine chest or he could injure himself by flying into a mirror. Use caution when taking your bird into the bathroom, and make sure his wings are clipped to avoid flying accidents.

KITCHEN

This is another popular spot for birds and their owners to hang out, especially around mealtime. Here again, dangers lurk for curious greys. An unsupervised bird could fly or fall into the trash can, or he could climb into the oven, dishwasher, freezer or refrigerator and be forgotten. Your bird could also land on a hot stove element, or he could fall into an uncovered pot of boiling water or a sizzling frying pan on the stove. The bird could also become poisoned by eating foods that are unsafe for him, such as chocolate, avocado or rhubarb.

LIVING ROOM

Are you sitting on your couch or in a comfortable chair as you read this book? Although it probably seems safe enough to you, your pet could be injured or killed if he decided to play hide-and-seek under pillows or cushions and was accidentally sat on. Your grey could become poisoned by nibbling on a leaded glass lampshade, or he could fly out an open window or patio door. By the same token, he could fly into a closed window or door and injure himself severely. He could become entangled in a drapery cord or a venetian blind pull or he could ingest poison by nibbling on ashes or used cigarette butts in an ashtray.

HOME OFFICE

This can be another playground, but you'll have to be on your toes to keep your pet from harming himself by nibbling on potentially poisonous markers, glue sticks or crayons, or injuring himself on push pins, pens or scissors that he finds irresistible as he investigates the pencil can on your desk.

OTHER AREAS OF CONCERN

If you have a ceiling fan in your house, make sure it is turned off when your bird is out of his cage. Make sure you know where your bird is before turning on your washer or dryer, and don't close your basement freezer without checking first to be sure your bird isn't in there.

Grey owners need to know that earrings and other jewelry prove to be great temptations to these birds. Pay attention if your bird suddenly takes an interest in your jewelry (chances are a sharp tug on your earring will warn you that this is happening) because your grey's inquisitive beak could destroy the jewelry, and the bird could swallow part of it and become ill. This is a good reason not to let your bird on your shoulder, but instead carry it so his head is at the level of your shirt pockets.

You do not need to keep your bird locked up in his cage all the time. On the contrary, all parrots need time out of their cages to maintain physical and mental health. I'm also not encouraging you to redecorate your home completely. What I'm trying to encourage you to do is to be aware of some of the dangers that may exist in your home and to pay attention to your bird's behavior so you can intervene before the bird becomes ill or injured.

Unfortunately, potential dangers to a pet bird don't stop with the furniture and accessories. A variety of fumes can overpower your grey, such as those from cigarettes, air fresheners, insecticides, bleach, shoe polish, oven cleaners, kerosene, lighter fluid, glues, active self-cleaning ovens, hair spray, overheated nonstick cookware, paint thinner, bathroom cleaners or nail polish remover. Try to keep your pet away from anything that has a strong chemical odor, and be sure to apply makeup and hair care products far away from your pet.

To help protect your pet from harmful chemical fumes, consider using some "green" cleaning alternatives, such as baking soda and vinegar to clear clogged drains, baking soda instead of scouring powder to clean tubs and sinks, lemon juice and mineral oil to polish furniture and white vinegar and water as a window cleaner. I use some of these products in my home to keep the environment a little friendlier for Sindbad, and I've found that these simple solutions to cleaning problems often work better than higher-priced, name-brand products.

PLANTS TO LOOK OUT FOR

Even common houseplants can pose a threat to your pet's health. Here are some plants that are considered **poisonous** to parrots:

- amaryllis
- bird of paradise
- calla lily
- daffodil
- dieffenbachia
- English ivy
- foxglove
- holly
- juniper
- lily-of-the-valley
- mistletoe
- oleander
- philodendron
- rhododendron
- rhubarb
- sweet pea
- wisteria

If you're considering a remodeling or home improvement project, think about your grey first. Fumes from paint or formaldehyde, which can be found in carpet backing, paneling and particle board, can cause pets and people to become ill. If you are having work done on your home, consider boarding your grey at your avian veterinarian's office or at the home of a bird-loving friend or relative until the project is complete and the house is aired out fully. You can consider the house safe for your pet when you cannot smell any trace of any of the products used in the remodeling.

I had some painting done and new carpeting installed before moving into my townhouse, and it took about three weeks for the odors to disappear completely. Fortunately, I could leave my bird at my old apartment while I moved items into the townhouse (making sure to keep all windows open whenever I was there to hasten the airing out process) and board her before the movers came to take the heavier items.

Having your home fumigated for termites poses another potentially hazardous situation to your pet grey. Ask your exterminator for information about the types of chemicals that will be used in your home, and inquire if pet-safe formulas, such as electrical currents or liquid nitrogen, are available. If your house must be treated chemically, arrange to board your bird at your avian veterinarian's office or with a friend before, during and after the fumigation to ensure that no harm comes to your pet. Make sure your house is aired out completely before bringing your bird home, too.

If you have other pets in the home that require flea treatments, consider pyrethrin-based products. These natural flea killers are derived from chrysanthemums and, although they aren't as long-lasting as synthetic substitutes, they do knock down fleas quickly

---

"SAFE" PLANTS

You're probably wondering which plants, if any, are considered **safe** to keep around pet birds. Here are some bird-safe plants:

- African violets
- aloe
- burro's tail
- Christmas cactus
- coleus
- edible fig
- fern (asparagus, Boston, bird's nest, maidenhair, ribbon, staghorn, squirrel's foot)
- gardenia
- grape ivy
- hen and chicks
- hibiscus
- jade plant
- kalanchoe
- palms (butterfly, cane, golden feather, Madagascar, European fan, sentry and pygmy date)
- pepperomia
- rubber plant
- spider plant
- yucca

and are safer in the long run for your pets and you. Or you can treat your dog or cat's sleeping area with diatomaceous earth, which is the crushed shells of primitive one-celled algae. This dust kills fleas by mechanical means, which means that fleas will never develop a resistance to it as they could with chemical products.

Closely supervise any interactions your grey has with other household pets.

Other pets can harm your grey's health, too. A curious cat could claw or bite your pet, a dog could step on him accidentally or bite him, or another bird could break his leg or rip off his upper mandible with his beak. If your grey tangles with another pet in your home, contact your avian veterinarian immediately because emergency treatment (for bacterial infection from a puncture wound or shock from being stepped on or suffering a broken bone) may be required to save your bird's life.

Owners and other people can unintentionally be a pet bird's worst enemy. At BIRD TALK, we frequently heard from distraught owners who accidentally rolled over on their pets while bird and owner took a nap together because the owner thought it would be cute to have the bird sleep with him or her. Another common problem grief-stricken owners alerted us to countless times was the danger of leaving nonstick cookware on the stove and having it boil dry because the person forgot about the pot. In the process, toxic fumes were released that killed a beloved pet bird.

Other owners would call, wanting someone to listen to their confession of accidentally stepping on a treasured pet or closing him in the refrigerator, freezer, washer or dryer. Fortunately, in the case of the appliance stories, the bird's disappearance was usually noted before any damage was done.

Enjoying

Your

part three

African
Grey

chapter 8

Understanding Your African Grey's Behavior

The following common avian behaviors are listed in alphabetical order to help you better understand your new feathered friend!

Attention-Getting Behaviors

As your grey becomes more settled in your home, don't be surprised if you hear subtle little fluffs coming from under the cage cover first thing in the morning. It's as if your bird is saying, "I hear that you're up. I'm up, too. Don't forget to uncover me and play with me!" Other attention-getting behaviors include gently shaking toys, sneezing or soft vocalizations.

Bat Bird

This is the term I use to describe a bird that enjoys hanging upside down from the curtains, drapery rods or inside her cage. Some greys are more prone to this behavior than others. It's perfectly normal, but a bit unsettling if you aren't ready for it! This is one way that grey's stretch, exercise and keep busy.

Beak Grinding

If you hear your bird making odd little grinding noises as she's drifting off to sleep, don't be alarmed! Beak grinding is a sign of a contented pet bird, and it's commonly heard as a bird settles in for the night.

Beak Wiping

After a meal, it's common for a grey to wipe her beak against a perch, on your sleeve (if your arm happens to be handy) or on the cage floor to clean it.

Birdie Aerobics

This is how I describe a sudden bout of stretching that all parrots seem prone to. An otherwise calm bird will suddenly grab the cage bars and stretch the wing and leg muscles on one side of his body, or she will raise both wings in imitation of an eagle. Again, this is normal behavior.

Your grey may look like she's doing calisthenics, but she's actually stretching.

Catnaps

Don't be surprised if you catch your grey taking a little catnap during the day. As long as you see no other indications of illness, such as a loss of appetite or a fluffed-up appearance, there is no need to worry if your pet sleeps during the day.

FLUFFING

This is often a prelude to preening or a tension releaser. If your bird fluffs up, stays fluffed and resembles a feathered pine cone, however, contact your avian veterinarian for an appointment because fluffed feathers can be an indicator of illness.

GROWLING

If your grey growls, it's because the bird is frightened of something in her environment that she's trying to scare away with the growling.

MUTUAL PREENING

This is part of the preening behavior described below, and it can take place between birds or between birds and their owners. It is a sign of affection reserved for best friends or mates, so consider it an honor if your grey wants to preen your eyebrows, hair, mustache or beard, or your arms and hands. If your grey wants to be preened, she will approach you with her head down and will gently nudge her head under your hand as if to tell you exactly where she wants to be scratched and petted.

Mutual preening is a sign of affection reserved for the most beloved friends or mates.

PAIR BONDING

Not only do mated pairs bond, but best bird buddies of the same sex will demonstrate some of the same behavior, including sitting close to each other, preening each other and mimicking the other's actions, such as stretching or scratching, often at the same time.

POSSESSIVENESS

Greys may become overly attached to one person in the household, especially if that same person is the one who is primarily responsible for their care. Indications of a possessive grey can include growling and other threatening gestures made toward other family members, and pair bonding behavior with the chosen family member.

You can keep your grey from becoming possessive by having all members of the family spend time with your bird from the time you first bring her home. Encourage different members of the family to feed the bird and clean her cage, and make sure all family members play with the bird and socialize her while she's out of her cage.

Keep your grey from becoming possessive by including all family members when socializing your pet.

PREENING

Preening is part of a grey's normal routine. You will see your bird ruffling and straightening her feathers each day. She will also take oil from the uropygial or preen gland at the base of her tail and put the oil on the rest of her feathers, so don't be concerned if you see your pet seeming to peck or bite at her tail. If, during molting, your bird seems to remove whole feathers, don't panic! Old, worn

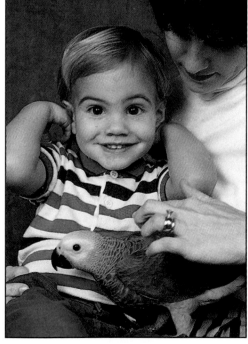

feathers are pushed out by incoming new ones, which makes the old feathers loose and easy to remove.

REGURGITATING

If you see that your bird is pinning her eyes, bobbing her head and pumping her neck and crop muscles, she is about to regurgitate some food for you. Birds regurgitate to their mates during breeding season and to their young while raising chicks. It is a mark of great affection to have your bird regurgitate her dinner for you, so try not to be too disgusted if your pet starts bringing up her last meal for you.

RESTING ON ONE FOOT

Do not be alarmed if you see your grey occasionally resting on only one foot. This is normal behavior (the resting foot is often drawn up into the belly feathers). If you see your bird always using both feet to perch, please contact your avian veterinarian because this can indicate a health problem.

SCREAMING

Well-cared-for greys will vocalize quietly (see separate entry for vocalization), but birds that feel neglected and that have little attention paid to them may become screamers. Once a bird becomes a screamer, it can be a difficult habit to break, particularly since the bird feels rewarded with your negative attention every time he screams. You may not see your attention as a reward, but at least the bird gets to see you and to hear from you as you tell her (often in a loud, dramatic way) to be quiet.

Remember to give your bird consistent attention (at least two hours a day); provide her with an interesting environment, complete with a variety of toys and a well-balanced diet; and leave a radio or television on when you're away to provide background noise, and your bird shouldn't become a screamer.

SNEEZING

In pet birds, sneezes are classified as either nonproductive or productive. Nonproductive sneezes clear a bird's nares (what we think of as nostrils) and are nothing to worry about. Some birds even stick a claw into their nares to induce a sneeze from time to time, much as a snuff dipper used to take a pinch to produce the same effect. Productive sneezes, on the other hand, produce a discharge and are a cause for concern. If your bird sneezes frequently and you see a discharge from her nares or notice the area around her nares is wet, contact your avian veterinarian immediately to set up an appointment to have your bird's health checked.

STRESS

This can show itself in many ways in your bird's behavior, including shaking, diarrhea, rapid breathing, wing and tail fanning, screaming, feather picking, poor sleeping habits or loss of appetite. Over a period of time, stress can harm your grey's health.

Provide your grey with a regular routine and lots of attention to decrease her stress.

To prevent your bird from becoming stressed, try to provide her with as normal and regular a routine as possible. Parrots are, for the most part, creatures of habit, and they don't always adapt well to sudden changes in their environment or schedule. But if you do have to change something, talk to your parrot about it first. I know it seems crazy, but telling your bird what you're going to do before you do it may actually help reduce her stress. I received this advice from avian behaviorist Christine Davis, and I explain what

I'm doing every time I've rearranged the living room on Sindbad or when I've had to leave her at the vet's office for boarding during business trips.

If you're going to be away on vacation, tell your bird how long you'll be gone, and count the days out on your fingers in front of the bird or show her a calendar.

Greys investigate new things by tentatively tasting or biting.

TASTING/TESTING THINGS WITH THE BEAK

Birds use their beaks and mouths to explore their world in much the same way people use their hands. For example, don't be surprised if your grey reaches out to tentatively taste or bite your hand before stepping onto it the first time. Your bird isn't biting you to be mean; she's merely investigating her world and testing the strength of a new perch using the tools she has available.

VOCALIZATION

Many parrots vocalize around sunrise and sunset, which I believe hearkens back to flock behavior in the wild when parrots call to each other to start and end their days. You may notice that your pet grey calls to you when you are out of the room. This may mean that she feels lonely or that she needs some reassurance from you. Tell her that she's fine and that she's being a good bird, and the bird should settle down and begin playing or eating. If she continues to call to you, however, you may want to check on her to ensure that everything is all right in your bird's world.

YAWNING

You may notice your grey yawning from time to time or seeming to want to pop her ears by opening her mouth wide and closing it. Some bird experts would say your bird needs more oxygen in her environment and would recommend airing out your bird room (be sure all your window and door screens are secure before opening a window or sliding glass door to let fresh air in), while other experts would tell you your pet is merely yawning or stretching her muscles. If you see no other signs of illness, such as forceful regurgitation or vomiting, accompanying the yawning, you have no cause for concern.

Feather Picking

One behavior African grey owners need to be aware of is feather picking because greys seem more prone to it than other parrot species. Don't confuse picking with normal preening. Once feather picking begins, it may be difficult to get a bird to stop. Although it looks painful to us, some birds find the routine of pulling out their feathers emotionally soothing. Greys that suddenly begin picking their feathers, especially those under the wings, may have an intestinal parasite called *Giardia*. If you notice that your bird suddenly starts pulling her feathers out, contact your avian veterinarian for an evaluation.

FEATHERED WARNINGS

One of the most fascinating things about your bird are her feathers. Your bird uses feathers for movement, warmth and balance, among other things. The following are some feather-related behaviors that can indicate health problems for your grey.

Fluffing: A healthy grey will fluff before preening or for short periods. If your grey seems to remain fluffed up for an extended period, see your avian veterinarian. This can be a sign of illness in birds.

Mutual preening: Two birds will preen each other affectionately, but if you notice excessive feather loss, make sure one bird is not picking on the other and pulling out healthy feathers.

Feather picking: A healthy bird will preen often to keep its feathers in top shape. However, a bird under stress may start to preen excessively and severe feather loss can result.

SINDBAD'S ROAD TO RECOVERY

For the first six years Sindbad lived with me, she picked her feathers regularly. She came to me without anything more than downy underfeathers from just below her lower beak to her vent, and her crop was picked down to only pink skin. Through a combination of factors, starting with improving her overall health and diet through introducing a variety of toys and establishing a calm, stable environment for her, eventually she learned to leave her feathers alone, though she still has a small bare area on her chest that may never be fully feathered because I believe she damaged the feather follicles themselves with her picking.

With lots of love and care, Sindbad is now a recovering feather picker.

What caused Sindbad to pull her feathers? Since I'm not her original owner, I can't answer that question. But during my investigations into feather picking, I learned that greys can pick for a number of physical or psychological reasons. Physical causes for feather picking can include skin or feather infections, internal or external parasites, liver disease, a poor diet or a hormonal imbalance.

Psychological causes for feather picking can include boredom, insecurity, breeding frustrations, nervousness or stress. Stress in a bird's life can result from something as simple as a rearrangement of the living room furniture to issues as complicated as bringing a new child or pet into the home.

After Sindbad's veterinarian determined that her picking had a psychological cause, I began to look at the world through her eyes. What seemed strange or frightening? What was comforting and familiar? What had owners of other birds that picked found successful in helping their pets stop this habit? I soon discovered I had many more questions than answers, but I pressed on.

I started by keeping Sindbad's environment as constant as possible. I had picked out a spot for her near a window in my apartment (a tradition that continues today, some six apartments later) and had arranged the rest of the living room accordingly before she arrived. I used the cage cover her previous owners had used to try to keep her surroundings familiar, although I housed her in a different, smaller cage that I thought was better suited to her physical condition and limited mobility. She never seemed distressed by the change in cages and settled right in to her new home.

After I established a stable home environment for my pet, I then set out to provide her with a predictable schedule. She knew when to expect breakfast and dinner, and she learned when I would be home from work. Because I allowed her plenty of time to adjust to her new home without any grand expectations from me, I didn't set her up to expect almost constant attention (which many new parrot owners do), then abandon her in favor of some other passing whim.

At first, I simply sat by her cage and talked quietly to her, then I'd leave the cage door open whenever I was home. She was free to come out of her cage if she wanted to, but she was equally welcome to stay inside if she felt more comfortable there. By the end of her first month with me, I could scratch Sindbad's head while she was in or on her cage. I didn't try to hold her or cuddle her, though, until she had been with me for several months because I was told by her previous owners that she wasn't a cuddler. Now, nine years later, the bird spends many evenings almost fused to my body (she's become that manageable) but only because I didn't rush her in the beginning.

After Sindbad was on a regular schedule and in a comfortable environment, I started to make her surroundings more interesting by adding variety to her diet and interesting toys to her cage. I offered corn on the cob, carrot sticks, zucchini wedges, pomegranate slices, green beans and pea pods in an effort to challenge her to work a little for her meals. I tried leather toys with lots of knots on them, wooden chew toys, cardboard paper towel rolls and plastic coffee stirrers woven between her cage bars in the hope that something would distract her from pulling her feathers. I hoped that between the toys and the food, she would find things to entertain herself with and that she would channel her energy into playing instead of using it to pull her feathers.

Much as I'd like to tell you differently, my efforts were neither overwhelmingly nor universally successful. Sindbad would leave her feathers alone for a week or so, then preen them down to the skin with a vengeance. Some weeks she would pull the feathers on her chest, while other weeks she would destroy the feathers on her back or the tips of her wings. It seemed for every two steps of progress, she took three steps backward into more serious picking. Still I persevered.

What I didn't try was any of the spray-on products touted to be cures for feather picking. Birds preen their feathers to keep them clean, so if you apply something to that feather, the bird is going to work extra hard to clean the feather, even to the point of chewing the feather off! If you're going to spray anything on your bird, make sure it's not any stronger than clean warm water, and also be sure your bird enjoys being misted before you make this a regular part of her routine.

I wasn't seeking a perfectly feathered bird for my efforts. I just knew that if she was still picking, something was still not right in her universe, and I continued to try to find out what was making her unsettled and insecure enough to keep picking.

As her health improved, Sindbad's picking lessened. One day, I happened to notice that I had a mostly feathered bird—after only six years of trying. I don't have a magic solution to offer except to ask that you have your bird evaluated by your avian veterinarian if she starts to pick, and if the cause isn't physical, please be patient with your feather-picking parrot as you try to distract her away from her feathers.

Petting Your Grey

Although African grey parrots are not renowned for being the cuddliest of parrots, they can learn to enjoy being petted and held. Among Sindbad's favorite spots to be petted are the nape of her neck, her head (especially if I ruffle her feathers gently against the grain), her eyelids and facial areas, the tips of her wings and wing folds, her crop, under her wings and at the base of her tail. She seems to enjoy having her beak rubbed and to have me gently pinch it with my thumb and forefinger.

If I'm petting her in an area she doesn't particularly want me to touch, she moves her head or body under my hand to show me the itchy spots. She also seems to like me to run my finger gently down her spine from her shoulders to the base of her tail. I've tried repeatedly to flip her over in my hand and rub her tummy, but she does not seem to enjoy this as much as having her head or neck petted.

chapter 9

Your Amazing African Grey

Taming Your Grey

Greys are remarkably sensitive birds that do not require a great amount of force or threat to discipline. Many times, all I need to do is speak sternly to Sindbad or give her what avian behaviorist Sally Blanchard calls "the evil eye" to get her to behave.

When disciplining your grey, remember that parrots are not "cause and effect" thinkers. If your bird chews on the molding under the cabinets in your home office, he won't associate you yelling at him or locking him in his cage with the original mis-behavior. As a result, most traditional forms of discipline are ineffective with parrots. You must be sure not to lose your temper with your bird and never hit him, even if the bird makes you very angry.

So what do you do when your grey misbehaves? When you must discipline your pet, look at him sternly and tell him, "No," in a firm voice. If the bird is climbing on or chewing something he shouldn't, also remove him from the source of danger and temptation as you tell him, "No." If your bird has wound himself up into a screaming banshee, sometimes a little "time out" in his covered cage (between five and ten minutes in most cases) does wonders to calm him down.

Once the screaming stops and the bird calms down enough to play quietly, eat or simply move around his cage, the cover comes off to reveal a well-behaved, calmed-down pet. In other cases, your screaming pet may just need to be reassured and held for a few minutes. With time and experience, you will soon be able to determine which types of screams require which type of response from you.

If your grey bites you while he's perched on your hand or if he begins chewing on your clothing or jewelry, you can often dissuade him from this behavior by rotating your wrist about a quarter-turn to simulate a small "earthquake." Your bird will quickly associate the rocking of his "perch" with his misbehavior and will stop biting or chewing.

TOILET TRAINING

Although some people don't believe it, greys and other parrots can be toilet trained so that they don't defecate on their owners. If you want to toilet train your bird, you will have to choose a word that will indicate the act of defecating to your pet, such as "go poop" or "go potty." While you're training your pet to associate the chosen phrase with the action when you see him about to defecate in his cage or on his playpen, you will have to train yourself to your bird's body language and actions that indicate he is about to defecate, such as shifting around or squatting slightly.

Once your bird seems to associate "go potty" with defecating, you can try picking him up and holding him until she starts to shift or squat. Tell the bird to "go potty" while placing him on his cage, where he can defecate. Once he's done, pick him up again and praise him for being such a smart bird! Expect a few accidents while you are both learning this trick, and soon you'll have a toilet-trained bird that you can put on his cage about every twenty minutes or so, give him the command and expect the bird to defecate on command.

Masterful Mimics

African greys not only whistle and sing, but they have also been known to carry on detailed conversations.

African greys are well known in the parrot world for their abilities to talk, whistle and sing. They can speak in a much wider range of voices than other parrots, and some have been known to carry on detailed conversations with themselves in several voices. African grey parrots are reportedly one of the best talking species in the parrot world. One bird, Prudle, had a vocabulary of 1,000 words when he retired from public life in 1977.

Although many greys learn to talk, none of them is guaranteed to talk. The tips offered below will help you teach your bird to talk, but please don't be disappointed if your pet never utters a word.

Training Tips for Talking

You will be more successful in training a grey to talk if you keep a single pet bird. Birds kept in pairs or groups are more likely to bond with other birds than to want to bond with people.

Start with a young bird because the younger the bird is, the more likely he is to want to mimic human speech. Keep in mind, though, that greys are notoriously late talkers. Other avian species may start to talk as early as six months of age, while grey parrots usually don't begin talking until they are more than a year old. Anxious owners often wonder if they have a "dud" in the talking department before the grey even has a chance to express himself!

Start Simple

Pick one phrase to start with. Keep it short and simple, such as the bird's name. Say the phrase slowly so that the bird learns it clearly. Some people teach their birds to talk by rattling off words and phrases quickly, only to be disappointed when the bird ignores them completely or repeats the words in a blurred jumble that cannot be understood.

Be sure to say the chosen phrase with emphasis and enthusiasm. Birds like a "drama reward" and seem to learn words that are said emphatically, which may be why some of them pick up bad language so quickly!

Try to have phrases make sense. For instance, say "Good morning" or "Hello" when you uncover the bird's cage each day. Say "Good-bye" when you leave the room, or ask "Want a treat?" when you offer your grey his meals. (Phrases that make sense are also more likely to be used by you and other members of your family when conversing with your bird. The more your bird hears an interesting word or phrase, the more likely he is to say that phrase some day.)

Don't change the phrase around. If you're teaching your bird to say "Hello," for example, don't say "Hello" one day, then "Hi" the next, followed by "Hi, Sindbad!" (or whatever your bird's name is) another day.

Keep Sessions Short

Keep training sessions about ten to fifteen minutes in length. Maintain eye contact with your bird through-out the training session. If you give your bird your full attention, he will return the favor, and both of you are likely to enjoy the training sessions more and benefit from them.

Train your bird in a quiet area. Think of how distracting it is when someone is trying to talk to you with a radio or television blaring in the background. It's hard to hear what the other person is saying under those conditions, isn't it? Your grey won't be able to hear you any better or understand what you are trying to accomplish if you try to train him in the midst of noisy distractions. Be sure to keep your grey involved in your family's routine, though, because isolating him completely won't help him feel comfortable and part of the family. Remember that a bird needs to feel comfortable in his environment before he will draw attention to himself by talking.

Remember to keep eye contact with your grey when you are communicating with him.

Be patient with your pet. Stop the sessions if you find you are getting frustrated. Your bird will sense that something is bothering you and will react by becoming bothered himself. This is not an ideal situation for you to train your pet or for your grey to learn in. Try to keep your mood upbeat. Smile a lot and praise your pet when he does well!

Graduate to more difficult phrases as your bird masters simple words and phrases. Consider keeping a log of the words your bird knows (this is especially helpful if more than one person will be working with the bird).

When you aren't talking to your grey, try listening to him. Birds sometimes mumble to themselves to practice talking as they drift off to sleep. See if you don't notice your grey muttering softly to himself after you've covered his cage in the evenings.

Do Tapes Work?

You're probably wondering if the talking tapes and compact discs sold in pet stores and through advertisements in bird magazines work. The most realistic answer I can give is "sometimes." Some birds learn from the repetition of the tapes and CDs that, fortunately, have gotten livelier and more interesting to listen to in recent years. Other birds benefit from having their owners make tapes of the phrases the bird is currently learning and hearing those tapes play when their owners aren't around. I would recommend against a constant barrage of taped phrases during the day, because the bird is likely to get bored hearing the same thing for hours on end. If he's bored, the bird will be more likely to tune out the tape and tune out the training in the process.

If your grey doesn't speak, he will find other charming ways to communicate with you.

Just because the species has a reputation for talking, though, doesn't mean that your bird will automatically speak. Sindbad had about a thirty-phrase vocabulary in her previous home, and she also sang songs and whistled several tunes. She has talked infrequently since coming to live with me, and has yet to sing a song or whistle a complete tune. I've accepted her for the charming creature she is, rather than expected her to be a chatty companion. She communicates with me using a series of squeaks, squawks and screams, and we seem to understand each other just fine.

Other Ways Greys Communicate

If your bird chooses not to talk, he may vocalize in other ways, such as imitating appliances or other birds. Sindbad has a repertoire that includes clicks and squeaks she must have learned in the wild, trash compactors, garbage disposals, slide whistles, microwave timers, a smoke detector with a low battery, hammering and two different sounds of whimpering puppies. The last two she's learned since living with me, as our neighbors were building a new porch one summer (the hammer) and she's been boarded on several occasions at the vet's office with puppies nearby. She is most likely to entertain me with her sound effects collection as she is drifting off to sleep at night or when I have the dishwasher going. I believe she thinks if I can make noise, then she can, too!

African greys tend to mimic their owners in many ways. You will find that your grey will vocalize when you are on the phone; eat when you eat; nap when you're engaged in a quiet activity, such as paying bills or writing letters; and sneeze or cough when you are under the weather. He will also

Your grey will get used to your routine and may even mimic your activities.

acclimate himself to your schedule rather quickly and may pick up on clues you think are quite subtle. As an example, Sindbad gets rather agitated whenever I brush my teeth because she has learned that this often means I'm about to leave her alone and go to work or to run errands.

When my day has ended and I'm settled down on the couch watching television, Sindbad settles down, too. After she's had her supper and her evening bowl of water, she knows that bedtime comes shortly thereafter. Some evenings she goes right to bed, while on other nights (especially when she feels she hasn't had enough attention during the day) she needs a little extra cuddling to help her unwind and get ready for bed.

part four

Beyond
the
Basics

chapter 10

Resources

Recommended Reading

For more information on bird care, look for these books at your local library, bookstore or pet store:

ABOUT HEALTH CARE

Doane, Bonnie Munro. *The Parrot in Health and Illness: An Owner's Guide.* New York: Howell Book House, 1991.

Gallerstein, Gary A. DVM. *The Complete Bird Owner's Handbook.* New York: Howell Book House, 1994.

Ritchie, Branson W. DVM, PhD, Greg J. Harrison DVM, Linda R. Harrison. *Avian Medicine: Principles and Application.* Lake Worth, Fla.: Wingers Publishing Inc, 1994.

ABOUT BREEDING

Gonzalez, Fran. *Breeding Exotic Birds: A Beginner's Guide.* Cypress, Calif.: Neon Pet Publications, 1993.

Schubot, Richard, Susan Clubb, DVM, Kevin Clubb. *Psittacine Aviculture.* Loxahatchee, Fla.: Avicultural Breeding and Research Center, 1992.

About Training

Athan, Mattie Sue. *Guide to a Well-Behaved Parrot.* Hauppauge, N.Y.: Barron's Educational Series Inc, 1993.

Hubbard, Jennifer. *The New Parrot Training Handbook.* Fremont, Calif.: Parrot Press, 1997.

About Pet Loss

Sife, Wallace PhD. *The Loss of a Pet.* New York: Howell Book House, 1993.

General Titles

Alderton, David. *Keeping African Grey Parrots.* Neptune, N.J.: TFH Publications Inc., 1995.

———. *You and Your Pet Bird.* New York: Alfred A. Knopf, 1994.

———. *A Birdkeeper's Guide to Parrots and Macaws.* Blacksburg, Va.: Tetra Press, 1989.

———. *A Birdkeeper's Guide to Pet Birds.* Blacksburg, Va.: Tetra Press, 1987.

Freud, Arthur. *The Parrot: An Owner's Guide to a Happy, Healthy Pet.* New York: Howell Book House, 1996.

Gonzales, Fran. *African Greys.* Cypress, Calif.: Neon Pet Publications, 1996.

Paradise, Paul. *African Grey Parrots.* Neptune, N.J.: TFH Publications Inc., 1979.

Pinter, Helmut. *African Grey Parrots as a Hobby.* Neptune, N.J.: TFH Publications Inc., 1995.

The Duke of Bedford. *Parrots and Parrot-like Birds.* Neptune, N.J.: TFH Publications Inc., 1969 (U.S. distribution).

Wolter, Annette. *African Grey Parrots: A Complete Pet Owner's Manual.* Hauppauge, N.Y.: Barron's Educational Series Inc., 1987.

Magazines

Bird Talk magazine, P.O. Box 57347, Boulder, CO 80322-7347.

Birds USA. Look for it in your local bookstore or pet store.

Caged Bird Hobbyist, 5400 NW 84 Ave., Miami, FL 33166-3333.

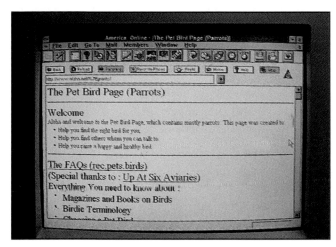

The Internet is a good resource for information on pet birds.

Online Resources

Bird-specific sites have been cropping up regularly on the Internet. These sites offer pet bird owners the opportunity to share stories about their pets, along with trading helpful hints about bird care.

If you belong to an online service, look for the pet site (it's sometimes included in more general topics, such as "Hobbies and Interests," or more specifically "Pets"). If you have Internet access, ask your Web browser software to search for "greys," "parrots" or "pet birds."

Videos

Alex the Grey. Avian Publications, 1653 Briardale Rd. NE, Minneapolis, MN 55432.

Care ı Breeding Series: African Greys and the Poicephalus Group. Avian Publications, 1653 Briardale Rd. NE, Minneapolis, MN 55432.

The Positive Approach to Parrots as Pets: Understanding Bird Behavior (tape 1) and *Training Through Positive Reinforcement* (tape 2). Natural Encounters Inc., P.O. Box 68666, Indianapolis, IN 46268.

Bird Clubs

The African Parrot Society
P.O. Box 204
Clarinda, IA 51632-2731.

The American Federation of Aviculture
P.O. Box 56218
Phoenix, AZ 85079-6128.

Avicultural Society of America
P.O. Box 5516
Riverside, CA 92517-5517.

International Avicultural Society
P.O. Box 280383
Memphis, TN 38168.

Society of Parrot Breeders and Exhibitors
P.O. Box 369
Groton, MA 01450.